ANGLICAN RELIGIOUS ORDERS AND COMMUNITIES

A Directory

**Prepared for the Decade of Evangelism
An Initiative of the Anglican
Communion Office**

Forward Movement Publications
Cincinnati, Ohio, USA

© 1991 Forward Movement Publications, 412 Sycamore Street, Cincinnati, Ohio 45202, USA

Preface

At the heart of the initiatives surrounding the Decade of Evangelism have been the faithful prayers of Christ's people, the church. In 1990 the religious orders were asked by the Primates Meeting to take part in this work of intercession. What more appropriate a vehicle than our own religious communities, whose primary calling is to a life of prayer. Thus, over the past months men and women in religious orders throughout the Anglican Communion have been using special prayer cards to help and inform them in their prayers for the Decade of Evangelism. This publication is a direct result of their involvement, and is an expansion of information already available on the Decade of Evangelism mailing list. Included in this directory are all the addresses and details that could be gathered from responses to a questionnaire sent to the community addresses available to the Anglican Communion Office in 1990.

The Anglican Communion is organized by province, a national church or geographical area incorporating several dioceses. However, for easier reference, generally, we have classified each religious order or Christian community by country. We have also indicated whether membership is open to men, women or both. The first address is the residence of the superior, whether or not it is regarded as the mother house. Branch houses or other community addresses in the same country are listed beneath the entry. Cross-references are made to countries containing dependent or related houses.

Membership figures vary. Some communities have given only the numbers of those in life vows, while others have included novices and those in temporary vows. Omission of a community simply means that at publishing time we had no information.

This directory was prepared by the Anglican Communion Office for the Decade of Evangelism in consultation with the Communications Department and was co-sponsored by the Church of England's Advisory Council on the Relations of Bishops and Religious Communities. The editor wishes to acknowledge especially the contribution of the Reverend Canon Sam Van Culin and the staff of the Anglican Communion Office, and Brother James Francis, LCB, who worked on the research and compilation of data.

Corrections and additions for future editions may be sent to the Anglican Communion Office using the form at the back of this directory.

Introduction

By Brother James Francis, LBC

Some people express surprise that there are religious orders in the Anglican Communion, believing that it is an expression of Christian life peculiar to Roman Catholicism. In fact, from our work on this directory, we have found there are over a hundred and fifty orders living in three hundred convents and monasteries throughout the Anglican Communion. There are also religious congregations and communities in the Evangelical, Lutheran and Orthodox Churches, the Religious Society of Friends (Quakers), and inter-denominational and ecumenical communities like Taize in France.

The restoration of religious life within Anglicanism has not been easy. After the dissolution of the monasteries about 1540 it took three hundred years for the first religious society to be re-established in the Church of England. This revival was assisted by the Oxford Movement, which rediscovered some of the catholic and sacramental elements of the Anglican tradition. Gradually, religious communities were established in other countries, and now members of religious orders offer a great variety of gifts and a rich tradition of prayer and spirituality to the whole of the Anglican Communion.

Members of religious or monastic orders live what is called the "religious life" and are often referred to simply as "religious." However, this directory distinguishes between "religious" and "monastics." The religious' life of prayer and work is based upon a commitment to the active or "apostolic" vocation in the world. It usually involves the three-fold religious vows of poverty, chastity (celibacy) and obedience.

Those who feel called to enclosed community life

normally profess a vow of stability to belong to the particular monastic house where they live. The three monastic vows are obedience, stability and conversion of life (which includes an intention to live in simplicity and chastity). Those who take the monastic vows are referred to as monks and nuns.* Members of other orders are simply referred to as "religious." We have distinguished between the two traditions by denoting monastic communities by the symbol MV and those communities who take the religious vows by the symbol RV.

Many people believe that religious, particularly monks and nuns, are people who are trying to escape life and shut themselves off from "the outside world." But the monastery is a microcosm of the world experienced in a spiritual sanctuary of prayer. The vows taken express positive aspects of self-giving to God, not negative renunciations. The rule of life may seem limiting, with its demands of application—perseverance in prayer, community life, study and work—but it outlines a way of life which is truly liberating for those who choose to enter a religious order.

Several forms of religious life can be found within the Anglican Communion. In addition to monastic and religious vocations exercised in community, there are dispersed societies, consecrated women who take a vow of celibacy, contemplatives-in-the-world, and hermits. We have included information on dispersed societies whose details were available to us, but felt it inappropriate to include details about religious living the solitary life. Contemplatives-in-the-world and hermits do not usually have facilities for accommodating guests and it is not their custom to advertise their whereabouts. Nevertheless,

---

*Some religious, although they live an enclosed monastic life, still are consecrated under the traditional religious vows (e.g., the Franciscan Community of St. Clare). In these cases the text refers to their monastic lifestyle and may refer to them as monks and nuns.

it would be a sad omission if we were not to acknowledge their "desert calling," perhaps the most ancient of all religious vocations. Their yearning "for God alone" is one which has inspired people of all faiths and every age; their intercessory prayer for those of us who remain in the world empowers us in all that we do.

In all the different lifestyles of religious in the consecrated life, we find a parable of the church of God working as one body, each member fulfilling a particular role for the well-being of the whole. I hope that this directory will go some way toward bringing the religious life of the Anglican Communion to the attention of those who have not yet discovered it and that it will enable more and more people outside the church to glimpse the beauty of a life consecrated to Our Lord Jesus Christ.

Key to Symbols and Abbreviations

B   BISHOP VISITOR, denoting that the community is under the jurisdiction of a bishop visitor, episcopal guardian, or protector. The bishop represents ecclesiastical authority and usually is a sign of diocesan recognition.

C   CANONICAL STATUS or recognition by council. Some provinces have an official co-ordinating body whose role is to support religious orders and other Christian communities and grant provincial recognition. This status can also involve the community's being subject to certain canons in ecclesiastical law. We have only had information from certain provinces regarding membership of such councils etc. (Canada, the Episcopal Church USA, England, Ireland, New Zealand, Scottish Episcopal Church, Southern Africa and Wales.)

MV   MONASTIC VOWS. Vows of obedience, stability and conversion of life (*conversio morum*) as in the traditional Benedictine formula.

RV   RELIGIOUS VOWS. Vows of poverty, chastity and obedience. These are also known as the three evangelical counsels.

BCP   Book of Common Prayer (Episcopal Church USA)

Spellings have, for the most part, been retained as submitted.

AUSTRALIA

Community of the Holy Name
Women
RV   B

The Community House
40 Cavanagh Street
Cheltenham, 3192,
Victoria
Australia

Founded in 1888 in Melbourne, the community's original apostolic work was to minister to needy women and children living in the slums of the city. By 1908 the community was formally constituted and began to set up branch houses. The emergence of the welfare state has meant that the pattern of institutional care has given way to more individual ministries, e.g. hospital and welfare chaplaincy work. The sisters run a guest house for retreats and can sometimes make their hermitage available in the convent grounds.

Habit: A skirt and blouse in blue/white/cream with cross on which is engraved IHS. A few sisters, including a small enclosed group, still wear a traditional habit.

Membership: 39

The Rev'd Mother: Sister Elizabeth Gwen, CHN

The Retreat House, 32 Cavanagh Street, Cheltenham 3192, Victoria, Australia

The Mission House, 136 Napier Street, Fitzroy 3166, Australia

The Sisters CHN, 5 Emerald Street, South Oakleigh, 3167, Australia

The Sisters CHN, 54 Young Street, Seacliff, SA, Australia

The Enclosed Sisters CHN, RMB 8600, Wangaratta Sth, Victoria, 3678, Australia

Sisters of the Incarnation
Women
RV   B

The House of the Incarnation
1 Codford Street
Elizabeth
South Australia 5112
Australia

The community was founded in the Diocese of Adelaide in 1981 as a contemporary expression of the religious life. In addition to parish work, the sisters are also involved in the network of the Diocesan Ministry of Spirituality.

Habit: Secular dress with SI cross
Membership: 2
Guardian: Sister Patricia, SI

Melanesian Brotherhood
Men
RV   B

c/o The Anglican Church
Lockhart River
Q 4871
Australia

Founded in 1926, the Brotherhood worked in areas where the gospel had not been preached and with lapsed Christians. The brothers now work with the local church and make temporary promises of obedience, poverty and celibacy.

Habit: White shirt and calico, white/black sash and medal
Membership: 6
Superior: The Section Elder Brother

See also Papua New Guinea and Solomon Islands.

Society of the Sacred Advent
Women
RV   B

Community House
34 Lapraik House
Albion
Queensland 4010
Australia

Founded in 1892. The sisters are called to prepare the way for Jesus first in their hearts and then in the world in which they live. The life of the sisters is a round of prayer, silence and work. They are an active apostolic community engaged in retreat work; chaplaincy ministry in schools, hospitals and to the elderly; parish and youth ministry.

Habit: Veil, grey dress, white blouse-style collar and SSA cross
Membership: 5
Superior: The Rev'd Mother Superior, SSA

Society of the Sacred Mission
Men
RV   B

St. Michael's Priory
PO Box 180
Diggers Rest
Victoria 3427
Australia
Tel: 03 740 1618

Founded in England in 1893. A religious community engaged in educational, pastoral, and missionary work.

Habit: Black cassock, scapular and hooded capuce with red girdle

Membership: 12
Superior: The Rev'd Fr. Colin Griffiths, SSM

St. John's Priory, 14 St. John's Road, Adelaide, South
Australia 5000, Tel: 08 223 2348
See also England and South Africa.

Order of St. Benedict—Camperdown
Men
MV   B

Benedictine Monastery
PO Box 111
Camperdown
Victoria 3260
Australia

The monks of Camperdown seek to live out the Rule of St.
Benedict with its balance of prayer, liturgy, study and
manual work. The community supports itself with income
made from its printery. Other means of support come
from small crafts such as the making of icons and pot-
pourri. The monks are engaged in work within the
enclosure and undertake counselling and spiritual
direction.

Habit: Black tunic and scapular with hood and belt.
Membership: 4
Prior: The Very Rev'd Dom Michael King, OSB

Community of St. Clare
Women
RV   B

Monastery of the Blessed Virgin Mary
Stroud
New South Wales 2425
Australia

The Stroud community was founded by three sisters from Freeland, CSCl in England, in 1975. The present mud brick monastery was chiefly built by voluntary labour in 1979-81. In addition to the life of prayer the sisters have an extensive ministry to guests who stay or visit for the day. The house is independent from the Poor Clares at Freeland.

Habit: Brown dress, girdle and crucifix; no veil
Membership: 3
Superior: Sister Angela, CSCl

Society of St. Francis
Men
RV B

The Rectory
4 Talinga Close
Windale
New South Wales 2306
Australia

The brothers began their ministry in Australia in 1965 and are part of the First Order of SSF. The brothers are called to a Franciscan life of prayer and evangelism. They are engaged in an active apostolate in parishes and with retreat work.

Habit: Brown habit with capuce and white rope with 3
    knots
Membership: 16
Provincial Minister: Br. Daniel, SSF

The Hermitage, Stroud, NSW 2425, Australia
See also Belize, England, Ireland, New Zealand, Papua New Guinea, Scotland, Solomon Islands, and USA.

Community of the Sisters of the Church
Women
RV   B

216 Mahoneys Road
East Burwood
Victoria 3151
Australia

Founded in London in 1870, the sisters are now organised into three provinces: UK, Canada and Australia-Pacific. Their rule points the sisters to a life of "mingled adoration and action."

Habit: Skirt, blouse, veil and cape
Membership: 5
Sister-in-charge: Sister Scholastica, CSC

CSC House of Prayer, Dondingalong, via Kempsey, New South Wales 2440, Australia
96 Hereford Street, Glebe, New South Wales 2037, Australia
9/422 Cardigan Street, Carlton, Victoria 3053, Australia
See also Canada, England, and Solomon Islands.

BANGLADESH (Church of Bangladesh)

Christa Sevika Sangha
Women
RV   B

Jobarpar P.O.
Barisal District
Bangladesh 8240

Founded in 1970, the sisters divide their day between prayer and service. They are semi-enclosed and undertake the running of a girls' hostel and a fish/shrimp farm in their grounds. The sisters are supported by the Oxford Mission.

Habit: White sari with veil, blue girdle and cross
Membership: 12
Superior: Sister Susila, CSS

Brotherhood and Sisterhood of the Epiphany
Mixed
RV   B

Bogra Road
PO Box 21
Barisal
Bangladesh 8200

The first brothers arrived in Calcutta in 1880 to work with students. At the end of the century some went to East Bengal, now Bangladesh, to care for village Christians. The sisterhood began in 1902 with a small school and some medical and pastoral work. The community is supported by the Oxford Mission and the Fellowship of the Epiphany.

Habit: White cassock and black girdle for brother, white
    habit with scapular and veil and SE cross for sisters
Membership: 8
Superiors: The Rev'd Fr. George Golding, BE, and The
    Rev'd Mother Joan, SE

BELIZE

Society of St. Francis
Men

Bishop Thorpe
PO Box 535
Belize City
Belize

See also Australia, England, Ireland, New Zealand, Papua New Guinea, Solomon Islands, and USA.

CANADA

Order of Agape and Reconciliation
Mixed

The Prince of Peace Priory
Box 960
Chemainus
BC V0R 1K0
Canada
Tel: (604) 246-9578

A contemplative and semi-monastic order for men and women regardless of marital status.   Sponsored by Anglicans, it is ecumenical in outreach, including Eastern Orthodox and Roman Catholic members.   It seeks a modern adaptation of the eremitical ideal and the cultivation of higher consciousness.

Prior General: The Rev'd Fr. Cyril, OAR
Prioress General: Sr. Mary-Michael, OAR

Company of the Cross — Alberta
Mixed
C

RR 5 Stony Plain
AB T0E 2G0
Tel: 403-848-2881

Founded in 1957 and established in Alberta in 1968, the company is a lay order of men and women, regardless of marital status, who follow a rule of life. The company operate a boarding school.

Contact: Simon Jeynes or Norma Adams

Order of the Holy Cross
Men
MC   B   C

Holy Cross Priory
204 High Park Avenue
Toronto
ON M6P 2S6
Canada
Tel: 416-767-9081

The order was founded in 1884, and the Canadian priory
was established in 1973. It is international, multi-racial
and multi-cultural. The contemporary Benedictine lifestyle
combines the monastic disciplines of corporate and
individual prayer, study, worship, work and ministry
with modern social understanding of collective and
individual responsibility.

Habit: White tunic with scapular and hood, plain black
    cross
Prior: The Rev'd Br. Brian Youngward, OHC

See also Ghana and USA.

Society of Our Lady St. Mary
Women
C

Bethany Place
PO Box 762
Digby
NS
B1V 1A0
Canada

Founded in 1979. Affiliated with the Community of the
Sisters of the Church. Members live a life of apostolic

outreach and prayer, conduct Bible studies, quiet days, youth programmes, and respond to local community needs.

Sisterhood of St. John the Divine
Women
RV   B   C

St. John's Convent
1 Botham Road
Willowdale
Ontario
M2N 2J5
Canada

Founded in 1884, the sisters undertake a life commitment to prayer and service in the context of community life. the community is engaged in vocational programs, retreats, workshops, church embroidery and offering guest accommodation and a book room.

Habit: Traditional length with choice of collar, veil (optional) and ebony cross with eagle emblem
Membership: 45
Superior: The Rev'd Mother, SSJD

St. John's Rehabilitation Hospital, 285 Cummer Avenue, Willowdale, Ontario M2M 2G1, Canada
Cana Place, 3333 Finch Avenue East, Scarborough, Ontario, M1W 2R9, Canada. A residence for more than forty elderly people.
St. John's Priory, 11717-93rd Street, Edmonton, Alberta T5G 1E2, Canada. Offers guest accommodation, retreats, aids in diocesan and parish work, and in inner city ministry.

Community of the Sisters of the Church
Women
RV   B   C

St. Michael's Convent
127 Burgundy Drive
Oakville
ON L6J 6R1
Canada
Tel: 516-844-9511

An international community founded in England in 1870; established in Canada in 1890. Offering a retreat and conference centre.

37 Father Biro Trail, St. Elizabeth Village, Hamilton, Ontario L9B 1T8, Canada, Tel: 416-575-8700
172 Bay Street South, No. 505, Hamilton, Ontario L8P 3H7, Canada
See also Australia, England, and Solomon Islands.

Western Society of the Common Life
Men
B   C

4655 Westsyde Road
RR 1
Kamloops
BC V2C 1Z3
Tel: 604 579 9150

A community established in 1975 with an emphasis on the life of prayer and the conducting of retreats.

St. Nicholas' Priory, c/o Synod Office, Diocese of Cariboo

Worker Brothers and Sisters of the Holy Spirit
Mixed
17 Merino Road
Peterborough
ON K9J 6M8
Canada

An international congregation for lay brothers and sisters and lay workers regardless of marital status. Members make a life commitment to a common rule which is Benedictine in orientation, but not lived in community. From a contemplative model of prayer, meditation, worship, the Eucharist, and a focus on the theological concept of being and the fruit of the Spirit, comes the action of mission and ministry in the local parish, the church and the world.

Canadian Director: Sister Carol Matthew, WSHS

See also USA.

DOMINICAN REPUBLIC

Community of the Transfiguration
Women

The Sisters of the Transfiguration
Apartado 128
San Pedro de Macoris
Republica Dominicana

See also USA.

ENGLAND

Community of All Hallows
Women
RV   B   C

All Hallows Convent
Ditchingham
Bungay
Suffolk
NR35 2DT
UK
Tel: 0986 892749

Founded in 1855. The sisters follow the Rule of St. Augustine and undertake a variety of different work.

Superior: The Rev'd Mother Pamela, CAH

Society of All Saints
Women
RV B C

All Saints' Convent
St. Mary's Road
Oxford OX4 1RU
UK
Tel: 0865 249127

The Society of All Saints' Sisters of the Poor was founded in 1851, with the support of the first vicar of All Saints', Margaret Street. The sisters serve the cause of the gospel through their worship and work: an old people's home, a children's hospice offering respite care for children with life-threatening or terminal illness, a drop-in centre for the homeless, an embroidery department, and a small guest house.

Habit: Blue dress and scapular, white collar, veil with white rim
Membership: 18
Superior General: The Rev'd Mother Helen, SAS

All Saints' House, 82 Margaret Street, London W1N 8LH, UK, Tel: 071 637 7818
See All Saints Sisters of the Poor, USA.

Sisters of Charity
Women
RV B C

The Convent
St. Agnes Avenue
Knowle

Bristol BS4 2HH
UK
Tel: 0272 775863

Founded in 1869. The rule is based on that given to the Daughters of Charity by St. Vincent de Paul in the 17th century in France.   The sisters give wholehearted commitment to Jesus Christ whose life is perfect charity, serving him in his needy members. They undertake care of those in need, young or old, through parish work, missions, and retreats, and also run a nursing home, near Plymouth, for the chronically sick. A retreat and conference centre near Las Vegas, Nevada, in the USA also acts as a base for sisters who work in prisons and a local care centre.

Habit: Navy blue jacket and skirt, white blouse and navy
     veil, SC cross
Membership: 24
Superior: The Rev'd Mother Mary Theresa, SC

6 North View, Castletown, Sunderland SR5 3AF, UK, Tel: 091 5160 406
81 Fore Street, Plympton St. Maurice, Plymouth PL7 3NE, UK, Tel: 0752 345918, 0752 336205 (nursing home)
See also USA and Wales.

Order of Cistercians — Ewell Monastery
Men
MV   B   C

Founded in 1966. Living a simple life of prayer and manual work.   Assistance provided for eucharistic celebrations for the nuns at West Malling Abbey.

Habit: Traditional
Membership: 2
Prior: The Rev'd Fr. Aelred Arnesen

Community of the Companions of Jesus the Good Shepherd
Women
RV   B   C

The Convent, West Ogwell
Newton Abbot
South Devon TQ12 6EN
UK
Tel: 0626 65337

Founded in 1920, within the Augustinian tradition, the sisters were originally involved in teaching and parish work. In 1939 they moved to South Devon where retreats and quiet days are held for clergy, parishes and groups. Guests are accepted for private retreats and spiritual refreshment. In addition to the Eucharist and four-fold office, the rule ensures that all sisters spend at least one and a half hours daily in prayer, Bible study and spiritual reading. The community is extended to oblates and associates.

Habit: Brown habit, scapular, black veil with white cap
        and collar, leather girdle and silver/wood CJGS cross
Membership: 21
Superior: Mother Evelyn Theresa, CJGS

Community of the Epiphany
Women
RV   B   C

Copeland Court
Truro
Cornwall
TR1 3DR
UK
Tel: 0872 72249

Founded in 1883. Limited accommodation is available in the convent. Private retreats can be arranged and quiet days are held regularly.

Superior: The Rev'd Mother, CE

Society of the Franciscan Servants of Jesus and Mary
Women
RV   B   C

Posbury St. Francis
Crediton
Devon
EX17 3QG
UK
Tel: 036 32 2304

Founded in 1930, the Society follow a life of prayer, work, hospitality etc. Guests are received and retreats conducted between Easter and October.

Superior: The Rev'd Mother, SFSJM

Community of the Glorious Ascension
Men
RV   B   C

The Priory
Lawley Village
Telford
Shropshire TF24 2PD
UK
Tel: 0952 504068

Founded by twin brothers (now the bishops of Truro and Lewes) in 1960, the community are called to unite a working life with that of a community life. The four-fold office gives a monastic flavour to the life within the priories.

Habit: Grey, with hood, leather belt and CGA maltese cross attached
Membership: 10
Prior: The Rev'd Br. Kenneth, CGA

Alswear Priory, S Moulton, North Devon, EX36 4LH, UK, Tel: 07697 244
The Priory, 38 Burnside Crescent, Langley, Middleton, Manchester M24 3NN, UK, Tel: 061 643 5775
Bishop of Lewes, Beacon House, Berwick, Polgate, East Sussex BN26 6ST, UK, Tel: 0323 870387
Bishop of Truro, Lis Escop, Truro TR3 6QQ, UK, Tel: 0872 862657

Community of the Glorious Ascension
Women
(See France)

Oratory of the Good Shepherd
Men
RV   B

Brighton Vicarage
87 London Road
Brighton BN1 4JF
UK
Tel: 0273 682960

Founded in 1913 by Cambridge dons, the Oratorians are a dispersed society like a secular institute. They are grouped in colleges for regular meetings, and undertake parish work, teaching etc. While the Oratorians are not under religious vows, as such, the rule requires not only poverty, celibacy and obedience but also "labour of the mind," in addition to a daily Eucharist, offices, and an hour's prayer. Oratorians endeavour to follow the example of Jesus the Good Shepherd. Companions and associates are attached to members of OGS.

Habit: Black/white cassock, scapular and girdle, OGS cross
Membership: 43
Superior: The Rev'd Fr. Dominic Walker, OGS

See also South Africa and USA

Community of the Holy Cross
Women
RV   B   C

Holy Cross Convent
Rempstone Hall
Rempstone
Nr Loughborough
LE12 6RG
UK
Tel: 0509 880336

Founded in 1857 for mission work, the community later adopted the Rule of St. Benedict. The sisters undertake providing quiet days and can offer limited accommodation for private retreatants.

Superior: The Rev'd Mother Mary Katharine, CHC

Society of the Holy Cross
Men

c/o 9 Eldon Road
Kensington
London W8 5PU
UK

The Society is a congregation of priests, founded in 1855, and is probably better known by the letters SSC from its Latin title *Societatis Sanctae Crucis*. Its present function remains what it has always been, teaching the catholic faith as received in the Church of England, pastoral work in parishes, and the cultivation of discipline and holiness among the clergy, and so to the church at large. Branches can be found in Australia, New Zealand, South Africa, USA, and Zambia.

Habit: Secular dress with SSC gold lapel cross
Membership: 800
Master: Canon C.G. Colven

See also New Zealand and USA.

Community of the Holy Family
Women
RV   B   C

Holmhurst St. Mary
Baldslow
St. Leonards-on-the-Sea
East Sussex TN37 7PU
UK
Tel: 0424 754000

Founded in 1898 mainly for educational work.   Since closing its school, St. Mary's, Baldslow, in 1981, it has restored its house so that it can be used for a wider range of religious and educational activities.   CHF provide accommodation for retreats, conferences, lectures, concerts etc. Sisters are available to discuss problems with visitors who seek help and advice. The community tries to keep a balance between the life of prayer and active work.

Habit: Blue tunic, scapular, white collar and black veil
    over white cap, girdle and silver CHF cross

Membership: 7
Superior: The Rev'd Mother Gwendoline, CHF

Society of the Holy Ghost
Men

c/o   Beech Tree Cottage
Cheriton Fitzpaine
Crediton
Devon EX17 4JJ
UK

Founded in 1921. A society of secular priests who feel called to celibacy and to promote this vocation, together with a disciplined life of devotion, study and canonical obedience to lawful authority, and of simplicity in the use of money.

Superior: The Rev'd Martin Gibbs

Community of the Holy Name
Women
RV   B   C

Convent of the Holy Name
Morley Road
Oakwood
Derby DE2 4QZ
UK
Tel: 0332 671716

Founded in 1865 in London. The Community moved to Worcestershire in 1887 and then to Derby in 1990. Worship and prayer are at the heart of its life. Sisters are involved in parish and mission work, retreats, looking after guests, work with the deaf, and visiting in hospitals and prisons. The Holy Name Fellowship is an extension of the life and witness of the community.

Habit: Grey
Membership: 54
Superior: The Rev'd Mother Mary Patricia, CHN

The Retreat House, 11 Abbey Square, Chester CH1 2HU, UK,
Tel: 0224 321801
St. Anne's House, 51 Leaper Street, Derby DE1 3NB
624 Welbeck Road, Walker, Newcastle upon Tyne NE6 3AB,
UK, Tel: 091 262 4265
Holy Name House, Ambleside Road, Keswick, Cumbria CA12
4DN, UK, Tel: 0596 72998
3 Manor Road, St. Helen's Auckland, Bishop Auckland, DL14
9EW, Tel: 0388 609857
St. Michael's, 53 Wimbourne Road, Radford, Nottingham
NG7 5PD, UK, Tel: 0602 785101
See also South Africa.

Order of the Holy Paraclete
Women
RV   B   C

St. Hilda's Priory
Sneaton Castle
Whitby
North Yorkshire
YO21 1RW
UK
Tel: 0947 602079

Founded in 1915 as an educational order. The life is
influenced by a mixture of Benedictine and Celtic
spirituality. The community is mainly engaged in teaching,
hospital and university chaplaincies, retreats, conferences
and missions.   Recently, at the request of the former
Archbishop of Canterbury, the community sent two sisters
to be a "praying presence" at Lambeth Palace where they
are a symbol of the special ministry religious have within
the Anglican Communion.

Habit: Light grey, black veil and girdle, OHP silver cross
Membership: 79
Prioress: The Rev'd Mother Alison, OHP

St. Hilda's School, Carr Hall, Sleights, Whitby, North
Yorkshire YO21 1RW, UK, Tel: 0947 810242
St. Michael's House, 15 Portman Street, Leicester LE4 6NZ,
UK
St. Oswald's Pastoral Centre, Woodlands Drive, Sleights,
Whitby, North Yorkshire YO21 1RY, UK, Tel: 0947 810496
Abbey Cottage, Rievaulx, York YO6 5LB, UK, Tel: 043 96209
7 Minster Yard, York YO1 2JD, UK, Tel: 0904 620601
Martin House, Grove Road, Clifford Wetherby, West
Yorkshire LS23 6TX, UK, Tel: 0937 843449
37 Derwent Road, Lancaster LA1 3ES, UK, Tel: 0524 65461
Beach Cliff, 14 North Parade, Whitby, North Yorkshire YO21
3JA, Tel: 0947 601968
Cottage 5, Lambeth Palace, London SE1 7JU, UK, Tel: 071
928 5407
See also Ghana, Scotland, and South Africa.

Community of the Holy Rood
Women
RV   B   C

Holy Rood Convent
10 Sowerby Road
Thirsk
North Yorkshire YO7 1HX
UK
Tel: 0845 522580

Founded in Middlesborough in 1854, the community
moved to Thirsk in 1979. The sisters have a supportive
ministry in the surrounding area and offer accommodation
for retreats and quiet for a small number of guests.
Sisters are available for counselling and guidance with
special reference to the life of prayer. The confraternity
includes a Second Order and friends.

Habit: Modern, blue/grey with darker blue veil (optional) and silver CHR crucifix

Membership: 7

Prioress: The Rev'd Mother Georgiana, CHR

Society of the Holy Trinity
Women
RV   B   C

Ascot Priory
Ascot
Berks SL5 8RT
UK
Tel: 03447 882067

Founded in 1845, the Society was the first religious order to be re-established in the Anglican Church. The order is based upon the Poor Clares and remains a contemplative community today. The sisters can offer self-catering and catered retreats.

Habit: Traditional, with white choir cloak
Membership: 5
Superior: The Rev'd Mother, SHT

Little Brothers and Sisters of Christ
Mixed
RV   B

c/o Beacon House
Berwick Station
Polegate
BN26 6ST
UK
Tel: 0323 870387

Founded in 1986 by a group of young people in Sussex, the community combine a contemplative prayer life with an apostolate of ordinary secular employment. Inspired by Charles de Foucauld they imitate Jesus as they try to live the gospel values of littleness, weakness, vulnerability and simplicity of life. Professed brothers and sisters live either in small communities (fraternities) or alone. Work includes missions, parish, ancillary and social work. Profession is by temporary vows (for three years) and promises for associates.

Habit: Blue denim hooded smock or full length habit (dark grey), caritas cross attached to black belt
Membership: 13
Animator: Br. James Francis, LBC

St. Botolph's Vestry, Aldgate, London EC3N 1AB, Tel: 071 283 1670/1950 (Br. James)
7 Blossom Walk, Hailsham, East Sussex, BN27 1TT, Tel: 0323 847224 (Sr. Margaret)
See also Uruguay and Ghana.

Sisters of the Love of God
Women
RV   B   C

Convent of the Incarnation
Fairacres
Oxford
OX4 1TB
UK
Tel: 0865 721301

Founded in 1906, SLG was the first Anglican religious community to be founded specifically for living the contemplative monastic life. The rule owes much to the Carmelite tradition, particularly St. Teresa of Avila and St. John of the Cross. A balance between the corporate and solitary aspects of the lives of the sisters parallels the balance between liturgical and non-liturgical prayer. In addition to the nuns there are also oblate sisters, priest associates, companions and a fellowship.

Habit: Traditional brown habit, rope girdle and black veil
Membership: 53
Superior: The Rev'd Mother Anne, SLG

Bede House, Staplehurst, Tonbridge, Kent TN12 OHQ, UK,
Tel: 0580 891262
Dudwell St. Mary, Burwash, Etchingham, Sussex TN19 7BE,
UK, Tel: 0435 882282
Convent of St. Mary and the Angels, Woodland Ave., Hemel
Hempstead, Herts HP1 1RG, Tel: 0442 256989

Company of Mission Priests
Men
B

St. Oswald's Clergy House
Brougham Terrace
Hartlepool
Cleveland
TS24 8EU
UK
Tel: 0429 273539

Founded in 1940. An association of priests who, so long
as they are members, remain unmarried and work in
simplicity of life, mainly in the brotherhood of clergy
houses.

Warden: The Rev'd K. Mitchell

Society of the Precious Blood
Women
RV   B   C

Burnham Abbey
Lake End Road
Taplow

Maidenhead SL6 0PW
UK
Tel: 0628 604080

Founded in 1905. Based on the rule of St. Augustine, the Society is a contemplative community which exists for the purpose of perpetual intercession for the church and all people. Sisters take a watch daily in the Abbey church.

Habit: Black habit and veil, white collar and cap, crucifix worn from wide red ribbon
Membership: 25
Superior: The Rev'd Mother Margaret Mary, SPB

St. Pega's Hermitage, Peakirk, Peterborough PE6 7NP, Tel: 0733 252 219 A House of prayer set up in 1981. Intercessory prayer at heart of life. Sisters available for listening/counselling.
See also South Africa.

Community of the Presentation
Women
RV   B   C

Convent of the Presentation
69A Seabrook Road
Hythe
Kent CT21 5QW
Tel: 0303 267329

Founded in 1927.

Community of the Resurrection
Men
RV   B   C

House of the Resurrection
Mirfield
West Yorks WF14 0BN

UK
Tel: 0924 494318

Founded in 1892, the community undertakes teaching, retreats and missionary work.   Currently, its principal work is the running of a theological seminary at Mirfield. The daily time-table consists of Holy Communion and a four-fold office. An extension of the life and ideals of the community exist through the Fraternity whose oblates, companions and associates are linked to the community by a special rule of life.

Habit: Black cassock and grey scapular, leather belt with CR crucifix attached
Membership: 48
Superior: The Rev'd Fr. Silvanus Berry, CR

Royal Foundation of St. Katharine, 2 Butcher Row, London E14 8DS, UK, Tel: 071 790 3540   Retreat house offering spiritual direction, counselling and group retreats.   Double community of CR and Sisters of the Church.
Emmaus, Prospect Row, Sunderland, Tyne and Wear SR1 2BP, UK
See also South Africa.

Community of the Resurrection
Women
RV   B

St. Peter's Bourne
40 Oakleigh Park South
London N20 9JN
UK
Tel: 081 445 5535

Founded in 1884 in Grahamstown, South Africa, the community follows the mixed life of prayer and work. Originally founded for education work in South Africa, work is now undertaken in a wider sense: parish retreats, quiet days, conferences etc.

Habit: Dove grey habit, white collar and black veil with
    white headband, Celtic CR cross
Membership: 32
Superior: Sister Mary Eleanor, CR

See South Africa for Mother House.

Society of the Sacred Mission
Men
RV   B   C

All Saints' Vicarage
Grange Road
Middlesbrough TS1 2LR
Tel: 0642 245035

Founded in 1893, the Society grew out of a small missionary college in South London. Its main work became the training of ordinands at Kelham in Nottinghamshire. The theological seminary closed in the 1970's. The Society now undertakes the training of pre-theological students at its house in Durham, and parish and mission work elsewhere.

Habit: Black cassock, hooded capuce with red rope girdle,
    and crucifix
Membership: 41
Director: The Rev'd Fr. Thomas Brown, SSM

St. Antony's Priory, Claypath, Durham DH1 1QT, Tel: 091 384 3747
Willen Priory, Milton Keynes MK15 9AA, Tel: 0908 663 749
112 Tower Green, Middlesbrough TS2 1RD, Tel: 0642 241633
4 Rita Avenue, Rusholme, Manchester M14 4HF
See also Australia and South Africa.

Community of the Sacred Passion
Women
RV   B   C

The Convent of the Sacred Passion
Lower Road
Effingham, Leatherhead
Surrey KT24 5JP
UK
Tel: 0372 457091

The community was founded by Bishop Frank Weston in 1911 and is an Augustinian missionary order. They moved to Effingham in 1984 and withdrew from Africa in 1991, leaving a daughter foundation of some 90 sisters to take over the two houses in Tanzania

Habit: Air Force blue habit and scapular, white collar and cap, black belt-girdle and short black veil, CSP crucifix
Membership: 44
Superior: The Rev'd Mother Gloria, CSP

The Convent, 14 Laing House, Walstead Road, Walsall, West Midlands WS5 4NJ, UK, Tel: 0922 644 267
48 A Ilford Hill, Ilford, Essex IG1 2AS, UK, Tel: 081 478 8092
6 Calais Street, Camberwell, London SE5 9LP, UK, Tel: 071 274 0777
All Hallows House, Rowen Road, Norwich NR1 1QT, UK
See Community of St. Mary of Nazareth and Calvary, Tanzania.

Community of St. Andrew
Women
RV   B   C

St. Andrew's House
2 Tavistock Road
Westbourne Park

London W11 1BA
UK
Tel: 071 229 2662

Founded in 1861 by Elizabeth Ferrard, the first deaconess in the Church of England. Members of the community work in parishes, chaplaincies, in the development of the diaconate or in any other diaconal ministry to further the work of the church. Non-ordained sisters may find their ministry in one of the caring professions. Fundamental work is prayer and evangelism. Associates follow a simple rule of life and with friends and companions support the sisters in many ways.

Habit: Navy blue, white collar and cap, black veil, belt or girdle, deacon/deaconess cross
Membership: 18
Superior: The Rev'd Mother Lillian, CSA

9/10 War Memorial Place, Harpesden Way, Henley-on-Thames, Oxon RG9 1EP, Tel: 0491 572894

Order of St. Benedict—Alton Abbey
Men
MV   B   C

The Abbey of Our Lady and St. John
Beech
Alton
Hampshire
GU34 4AP
UK
Tel: 0420 62145

Founded in 1884, originally as the Order of St. Paul, its task was to care for retired seamen. After adopting the traditional Benedictine vows and rule the community now undertake retreat work and occasional parish work.

Habit: Black tunic, scapular with hood, and cloth
waistband
Membership: 12
Abbot: The Rt. Rev'd Dom Giles Hill, OSB

Order of St. Benedict—Burford Priory
Mixed
MV   B   C

Priory of Our Lady
Burford
Oxon OX8 4SQ
UK
Tel: 099 382 3141/3605

The sisters of the Society of the Salutation of Blessed
Mary the Virgin, a contemplative Benedictine community,
were founded in 1941 and moved to Burford in 1949. In
1987 the novitiate was also opened to men and the
community has evolved as a double monastery. In the
ordering of the day, priority is given to the worship of God
in word and sacrament, and to silent prayer. The monks
and nuns seek to support themselves by a variety of work
including printing, writing, counselling and the mounting
of icon-prints. A plantation of Christmas trees is maintained
as well as a small dried flower business. External
engagements are not normally undertaken. The
confraternity extends to oblates and friends.

Habit: Black tunic with scapular (which for the brothers
includes a hood), leather girdle; black veil and white
wimple for sisters
Membership: 8
Prioress: The Very Rev'd Dame Mary Bernard Taylor,
OSB

Order of St. Benedict—Edgeware Abbey
Women
MV   B   C

Convent of St. Mary at the Cross
Hale Lane
Edgeware
Middlesex HA8 9PZ
UK
Tel: 081 958 7868

A Benedictine community founded in 1866. Dedicated to stand with Mary, the mother of Jesus, at the cross, thus sharing in her commitment to embrace all people in Christ's love. While this is primarily a work of prayer, Christ's own compassion is seen to flow out into caring for the sick, disabled and aged in a residential care home situated within the enclosure. The community welcome all who wish to share their life; seeking God in tranquility and peace, including those of other faiths, Daily Eucharist and four-fold office. Vespers in Latin plainsong. Oblates and friends.

Habit: Black tunic and scapular with modernised headdress, black veil and leather girdle
Membership: 14
Abbess: The Rt. Rev'd Dame Rosemary Breeze, OSB

Order of St. Benedict—Elmore Abbey
Men
MV   B   C

Elmore Abbey
Church Lane
Speen
Newbury
Berkshire RG13 1SA

UK
Tel: 0635 33080

The Benedictine community of Our Lady and St. Benedict is a monastic order founded in 1914 at Pershore, which moved to Nashdom Abbey in 1926. It has been resited at Elmore since 1987. On Sundays and festivals the community attend the parish Eucharist. Otherwise, Mass is celebrated daily in the monastic oratory with a seven-fold office. Various pastoral works are undertaken, including retreats and days of prayer. The confraternity includes over 350 oblates as well as associates.

Habit: Black tunic, scapular with hood, leather girdle
Membership: 10
Abbot: The Rt. Rev'd Dom Basil Matthews, OSB

Order of St. Benedict—West Malling Abbey
Women
MV   B   C

The Abbey
West Malling
Kent
ME19 6JX
UK
Tel: 0732 843309

Founded in 1891, the first sisters engaged themselves in parish work among the poor in London. In 1906 they withdrew to Somerset to explore the Benedictine life and, in 1916, moved to West Malling. This was a Benedictine foundation c.1090 and some of the original pre-Reformation community buildings are still used today. The community is enclosed, seeking God in liturgical and personal prayer, manual work, study and the common life. The nuns welcome some 2,000 guests annually at the guest house.

They also grow most of their own organic vegetables and fruit. Other activities: keeping bees, craftwork, and printing.

Habit: Black tunic, scapular, veil and leather girdle with white wimple and headband
Membership: 29
Abbess: The Rt. Rev'd the Mother Abbess, OSB

Community of St. Clare
Women
RV   B   C

St. Mary's Convent
Freeland
Oxford OX7 2AJ
UK
Tel: 0993 881225

Founded in 1950 as the Second Order of the Franciscans, the sisters are called to a life of contemplative prayer within the enclosure. The community earns its living as far as possible by printing and by baking communion wafers. It also runs a small guest house which is well used for retreats and by other guests. It has a good many ecumenical contacts. Most of the sisters' fruit and vegetables are grown in the convent garden.

Habit: Brown habit, white cap, black veil and rope girdle
Membership: 11
Superior: The Rev'd Mother Patricia, CSCl

Community of St. Denys
Women
RV   B   C

St. Denys Convent
Vicarage Street
Warminster

Wiltshire BA12 8PC
UK
Tel: 0985 213020
         0985 214824 (Retreat Centre)

Founded in 1879 to undertake missionary work at home and abroad, the community now carry out their work through prayer, intercessions, retreat-mission work, adult education and parish work. The rule is a modification based on the Rule of St. Augustine. Confraternity includes oblates, associates and friends.

Habit: Blue habit and girdle, white collar and black veil,
         cross and profession ring
Membership: 16
Superior: The Rev'd Mother Frances Anne, CSD

Order of St. Elizabeth of Hungary
Women
RV   B   C

St. Mary's Retreat
Tilsmore Road
Heathfield
East Sussex
TN21 0XT
Tel: 043 52 3253

Founded in 1913 as an inner group of the Confraternity of the Divine Love. The order follows a Franciscan spirituality and rule. In 1970 the mother house was moved from London to Heathfield, which had previously simply been the guest and retreat house. Occasional parish retreats are undertaken and private retreatants and other guests are welcome.

Habit: Grey, with scapular, white collar and cap, black
         veil, brown girdle with three knots, OSEH cross with
         silver heart

Membership: 4
Superior: The Rev'd Mother Rachel, OSEH

Community of St. Francis
Women
RV   B   C

Compton Durville Manor House
South Petherton
Somerset TA13 5ES
UK
Tel: 0460 40473

Founded in 1909, the sisters moved to Somerset in 1962 and are now engaged in conference and retreat work, evangelistic and caring work. Affiliated to the Society of St. Francis, they also have double houses with SSF brothers in Stepney and in Belfast.   Tertiaries and companions share in their Franciscan life and ministry.

Habit: Brown habit with white rope with three knots,
    metal crucifix worn from girdle (optional)
Membership: 31
Provincial Minister: Sister Nan, CSF

St. Elizabeth's House, 33 Hampton Road, Birmingham B6 6AN, UK, Tel: 021 523 0215
10 Halcrow Street, Stepney, London E1 2EP, UK, Tel: 071 247 6233
Greystones St. Francis, First Avenue, Porthill, Newcastle under Lyme ST5 8QX, UK, Tel: 0782 636839
43 Endymion Road, Brixton, London SW2 2BU, UK, Tel: 081 671 9401
The House of the Divine Compassion, 42 Balaam Street, Plaistow, London E13 8AQ, UK, Tel: 071 476 5189
See also New Zealand and USA.

Society of St. Francis
Men
RV   B   C

St. Francis House
Normanby Road
Scunthorpe
South Humberside DN15 6AR
UK
Tel: 0724 853899

The society was founded in 1922 and comprises a First Order for men (SSF) and women (CSF), an enclosed sisterhood (CSCl) and a Third Order for clergy and laity. The brothers are called to a Franciscan life which has prayer and worship as its foundation. They engage in active work for the underprivileged, and work in parishes, schools, universities, retreats etc.

Habit: Brown tunic, capuce and hood, white rope with
    three knots
Membership: 187
Minister General: Br. Brian, SSF

The Friary, Hilfield, Dorchester, Dorset DT2 7BE, UK, Tel: 030 03 345/6
St. Francis House, 15 Botolph Lane, Cambridge CB2 3RD, UK, Tel: 0223 353 903
St. Mary at the Cross, Glasshampton, Shrawley, Worcestershire WR6 6TQ, UK, Tel: 0299 896345
The Friary, Almouth, Alnwick, Northumberland NE66 3NJ, UK, Tel: 0665 830213
St. Francis House, 113 Gillot Road, Birmingham B16 0ET, UK, Tel: 021 454 8302
St. Francis House, 68 Laurel Road, Liverpool L7 0LW, UK, Tel: 051 263 8581
St. Francis School, Hooke, Beaminster, Dorset DT8 3NY, UK, Tel: 0308 862 260

The House of Divine Compassion, 42 Ealaam Street, London E13 8AQ, UK, Tel: 071 476 5189

10 Halcrow Street, Stepney, London E1 2EP, UK, Tel: 071 247 6233

Holy Trinity House, Orsett Terrace, Paddington, London W2 6AH, UK, Tel: 071 723 9735

Shepherd's Law, Alnwick, Northumberland NE66 2DZ, UK

St. Michael's House, Solho Avenue, Handsworth, Birmingham B18 8BH, UK, Tel: 021 554 3521

See also Australia, Belize, Ireland, New Zealand, Papua New Guinea, Scotlalnd, Solomon Islands, and USA.

Community of St. John Baptist
Women
RV B C

Convent of St. John Baptist
Hatch Lane
Clewer
Windsor
Berkshire SL4 3QR
UK
Tel: 0753 850618

Founded in 1852, the community's life and work revolves around the daily Eucharist, private prayer, spiritual reading and a six-fold Divine Office. By combining a life of active work and prayer the sisters endeavour to fulfill their call to serve Christ in those who visit the convent. CSJB runs a retreat house, a home for elderly women, makes vestments, and does parish work. The community have an American affiliation in Mendham, New Jersey, with whom visits are exchanged. In 1980 the Community of Reparation to Jesus in the Blessed Sacrament moved into the convent to share the life and work of CSJB.

Habit: CSJB cross on red cord with black habit and veil, white collar and headband

Membership: 25 and 7 CRJBS Sisters
Superior: The Rev'd Mother Edna Frances, CJSB

Community of St. John the Divine
Women
RV   B   C

St. John's House
652 Alum Rock Road
Birmingham B8 3NS
UK
Tel: 021 327 4174

Founded in 1848 as a community of nursing sisters. The spirituality of CSJD is based upon St. John's Gospel – the apostle of love who was at the foot of the cross. Six sisters worked as nurses with Florence Nightingale during the Crimean War, and the community founded the first school of nursing in modern Britain. Today while some sisters still nurse, others are involved in the wider context of the ministry of healing, wholeness and reconciliation.

Habit: Royal blue dress and scapular, with short white veil and collar, CSJD cross with eagle of St. John in centre
Membership: 17
Superior: The Rev'd Mother Margaret Angela, CSJD

St. Peter's House, 308 Kennington Lane, London SE11 5HY, UK, Tel: 071 587 0087

Society of St. John the Evangelist
Men
RV   B   C

St. Edward's House
22 Great College Street
London SW1P 3QA

UK
Tel: 071 222 9234

Founded in 1866, it was the first religious order for men established in the Anglican Communion. The community at Westminster are engaged in hospitality, retreats, spiritual direction, missions, and work with the homeless. The confraternity extends to a Fellowship of St. John.

Habit: Black cassock and rope with three knots
Membership: 19
Superior: The Rev'd Fr. James Naters, SSJE

The Anchorhold, 35 Paddockhall Road, Haywards Heath, Sussex, RH16 1HN, Tel: 0444 452468
The Priory, 228 Iffley Road, Oxford, OX4 1SE, Tel: 0865 248116
See also USA.

Community of St. Katherine
Women
RV   B   C

St. Katherine's Convent
Parmoor
Henley-on-Thames
Oxon RG9 3NN
UK
Tel: 0494 881272

Founded in 1879. An Augustinian order which provides a home for elderly women. Private retreats and conducted day retreats can also be offered.

Habit: Traditional
Membership: 4
Superior: The Rev'd Mother Christine, CSK

Community of St. Laurence
Women
RV   B   C

Convent of St. Laurence
Belper
Derbyshire
DE5 1DP
Berkshire SL4 3QR
UK
Tel: 077 382 2585

Founded in 1874, the Community's main work is the care of elderly women.   The house is developing work with private guests who come for retreats, rest and study. Associates support the Community with daily prayer.

Habit: Traditional, with cross
Membership: 10
Superior: The Rev'd Mother Kathleen Mary, CSL

Society of St. Margaret—East Grinstead
Women
RV   B   C

St. Margaret's Convent
East Grinstead
West Sussex
RH19 3LE
UK
Tel: 0342 323497

Founded in 1855, the community undertakes nursing and parish work, runs guest houses and a home for the elderly. Jesus in the Blessed Sacrament is central to the sisters' life of prayer. Each day every sister takes part in a watch before the Sacrament, at least one and a half hours private prayer and Bible reading, a four-fold office, and the Eucharist. Men and women who wish to share in the dedication of the sisters may become associates. SSM East Grinstead and its branch houses form part of the larger Society of St. Margaret, which includes three other autonomous convents, in Aberdeen, Scotland; Haggerston, London; and Boston, USA. As well as their religious vows the sisters make a vow of charity.

Habit: Grey with scapular, black veil and belt-girdle,
    black wooden cross with white inset
Membership: 36
Superior: The Rev'd Mother Raphael Mary, SSM

Neale House, (Conference and Retreat Centre), Moat Road, East Grinstead, West Sussex RH19 3LB, UK, Tel: 0342 312552
St. Mary's Convent & Nursing Home, Burlington Lane, Chiswick, London W4 2QF, UK, Tel: 081 994 4641
Trinity House, 20 Windlesham Road, Brighton, West Sussex BN1 3AG, UK, Tel: 0273 735322
See also Haiti, Scotland, Sri Lanka, and USA.

Society of St. Margaret—St. Saviour's Priory
Women
RV   B   C

St. Saviour's Priory
18 Queensbridge Road
Haggerston
London E2 8NS
Tel: 071 739 6775/9976

This priory is one of the four autonomous convents which comprise the Society founded by John Mason Neale at East Grinstead in 1855. The first sisters came to Haggerston in 1866 to nurse and work in the local community. The daily Eucharist, five-fold office and one and a half hours' private prayer form the basis for work undertaken by the sisters. The priory has a few guest rooms and facilities for private retreats for both men and women.

Habit: Grey tunic and scapular, white collar, black veil with white rim, SSM wooden cross
Membership: 30
Superior: The Rev'd Mother Mary Teresa, SSM

Priory of Our Lady, Walsingham, Norfolk NR22 6ED, UK, Tel: 0328 820340 The Sisters at Walsingham are engaged in work at the Shrine of Our Lady and also in parish work locally.
See also Haiti, Scotland, Sri Lanka, and USA.

Community of St. Mary the Virgin
Women
RV   B   C

St. Mary's Convent
Challow Road
Wantage
Oxon OX12 9DJ
UK
Tel: 023 573 7112

Founded in 1848. The community's rule is derived from the Rule of St. Augustine, influenced by St. Francis de Sales. Thus the community live the "mixed" life: the way of Martha and Mary. Sisters preach, conduct schools of prayer, retreats, and are involved in care work and neighbourhood ministry. Two members of the community are hermits. There are nearly 200 oblates, men and women, living under a rule, and also about 600 associates.

Habit: Black-blue-grey dress or traditional habit, black veil with white cap and collar, silver CSMV cross and ring
Membership: 120
Superior General: The Rev'd Mother Allyne, CSMV

23 Old Town, Clapham, London SW4 0JT, Tel: 071 622 5733
Neighbourhood ministry
Spelthorne St. Mary, 55 Milton Road, Harpenden, Herts AL5
5NX, Tel: 0582 768511 Rehabilitation of alcoholics and drug
abusers
White Lodge, Denchworth Lane, Wantage, Oxon OX12 9AU,
Tel: 023 572 377 Neighbourhood ministry
St. Katherine's House, Ormond Road, Wantage, Oxon OX12
8EA, Tel: 023 572 739 Home for the elderly
Glebe House, Childrey, Wantage, Oxon OX12 9UP, Tel: 023
559 678
St. Mary's Lodge, Challow Road, Wantage, Oxon OX12 9DJ,
Tel: 023 576 141 Neighbourhood ministry
See also South Africa.

Community of St. Peter
Women
RV   B   C

St. Peter's Convent
Maybury Hill
Woking
Surrey GU22 8AE
UK
Tel: 0483 761137

Founded in 1861. CSP is Augustinian, undertaking
retreat work and conferences within the convent grounds.

Habit: Blue full length habit with CSP cross and black
    veil
Membership: 23
Superior: The Rev'd Mother Margaret Paul, CSP

St. Columba's House (address as above), Tel: 0483 766 498

Community of St. Peter—Horbury
Women
RV   B   C

St. Peter's Convent
Dovecote Lane
Horbury
Wakefield
West Yorkshire WF4 6BB
UK
Tel: 0924 272181

Founded in 1858 and based on the Rule of St. Benedict, the sisters undertake retreats and mission work. The community have recently moved from the large convent and are now looking for a new site.

Habit: Black tunic and scapular with girdle, white collar and black veil with white lining, silver crucifix
Membership: 13
Superior: The Rev'd Mother Phyllis, CSPH

Community of St. Wilfrid
Women
RV   B   C

St. Wilfrid
5 Culverland Close
Exeter
Devon EX4 6HR
UK
Tel: 0392 35538

Founded in 1866, the sisters form a Benedictine community which has a co-educational school in Exeter.

Superior: The Rev'd Mother, CSW

Community of the Servants of the Cross
Women
RV   B   C

Convent of the Holy Rood
Lindfield
Haywards Heath
Sussex RH16 2RA
UK
Tel: 044 47 2345

A community of Augustinian sisters founded in 1882, the sisters were originally engaged in caring for the chronically sick and infirm. Now the convent provides accommodation for a day centre, visitors making retreats, and for church groups of all denominations.

Habit: Black tunic, scapular and veil with white wimple and headband, black-white CSC cross
Membership: 12
Superior: The Rev'd Mother Superior

Community of the Servants of the Will of God
Men
MV   B   C

Monastery of the Holy Trinity
Crawley Down
Crawley
West Sussex RH10 4LH
UK
Tel: 0342 712074

CSWG is a contemplative community founded in 1953. It is committed to restoring the church within its essential tradition of worship, faith and conversion of life, particularly with uniting the contemplative and liturgical traditions of the churches east and west. The daily life is based upon a simple pattern of corporate prayer, silence, work and periods of reading and solitary prayer in the monks' cells. The community occupy 60 acres of woodland and simple farmland. Membership is extended to associates.

Habit: Hooded denim knee-length smock, leather belt
    with bronze CSWG cross attached; albs worn in choir
Membership: 10
Superior: The Rev'd Fr. Gregory Wilkins, CSWG

Monastery of Christ the Saviour, 23 Cambridge Road, Hove,
East Sussex, BN3 1DE, UK, Tel: 0273 726698

Society of the Sisters of Bethany
Women
RV   B   C

7 Nelson Road
Southsea
Hampshire
PO5 2AR
UK
Tel: 0962 833498

Founded in 1866.   The community now live in three
houses and provide opportunities for retreats and quiet
days.   Parish work and missions are also undertaken.
The rule is based on the spirituality of the Visitation
order.

Habit: Blue tunic and scapular with girdle and cross
    attached, short black veil
Membership: 21
Superior: The Rev'd Mother Christina Mary, SSB

114 Christchurch Road, Winchester, Hampshire SO23 9TG,
UK, Tel: 0962 68694

Community of the Sisters of the Church
Women
RV   B   C

St. Michael's Convent
56 Ham Common
Richmond

Surrey TW10 7JH
UK
Tel: 081 940 8711 and 081 948 8502

The Community was founded in 1870 in London by Emily
Ayckbown, who had begun work for the poor of her
father's parish in Chester some years earlier. She placed
the Community under the patronage of Michael and the
Angels, pointing the sisters to a life of "mingled adoration
and action," of contemplation and active ministry.   In
recent years CSC has gradually divested itself of its many
institutions but continues to find ways of incarnating its
original call, *Pro Ecclesia Dei*, to worship and ministry for
the whole people of God.   CSC is organised into three
provinces, UK, Canada and Australia-Pacific.

Habit: Green cape and skirt, with white top and black
    veil; habit optional, but CSC Celtic cross always worn
Membership: 71 (31 in UK)
Superior: The Rev'd Mother Judith, CSC

St. Gabriel's, 27A Dial Hill Rd, Clevedon, Avon BS21 7HL,
UK, Tel: 0272 872586
The Royal Foundation of St. Katherine's, 2 Butcher Row,
London E14 8DS, UK, Tel: 071 790 3540 Retreats and quiet
days and spiritual direction
See also Australia, Canada, and Solomon Islands.

FIJI

Community of the Sacred Name
Women

St. Christopher's Home
Box 8232
Nakasi
Suva
Fiji

A house of prayer and children's home.

See also New Zealand.

FRANCE

Community of the Glorious Ascension
Women
RV   B   C

Prasada
Quartier Subrane
Montauroux
83440 Fayence
Var
France

The sisters are called to unite a working life in ordinary jobs outside their priories with a monastic community life. The sisters recently moved from Wandsworth, England, to France.

Habit: Secular dress with CGA cross
Membership: 2
Prioress: Sister Jean, CGA

See also England.

GHANA

Order of the Holy Cross
Men
MV   B

Philip Quaque Monastery & Novitiate
PO A200 Adisadel
Cape Coast
Ghana

A monastic community founded in 1884, adopting the traditional Benedictine vows in 1987. The Order aims to interpret Benedictine spirituality in a way appropriate for an active apostolate in the modern world.

Habit: White tunic, scapular with hood, and plain black cross
Membership: 45
Superior: The Rev'd Father Prior, OHC

See also Canada and USA.

Order of the Holy Paraclete
Women
RV   B   C

PO Box 594
Accra
Ghana

Founded in England in 1915 as an educational order, the sisters' spirituality is influenced by a mixture of Benedictine and Celtic traditions.

Habit: White dress with roll-neck collar
Membership: 3

See also Scotland, South Africa, and England.

Little Brothers of Christ
Men
RV   B

PO Box 300
Bolgathanga
Ghana

Founded in England in 1986, the order in Ghana began in 1990. The spirituality is based upon Charles de Foucauld who strove to serve Christ in the poor.

Habit: Secular dress with simple wooden cross
Contact: The Rev'd Fr. Edwin Abanga, LBC

See also England and Uruguay.

HAITI

Society of St. Margaret
Women
RV   B

St. Margaret's Convent
Box 857
Port-au-Prince
Haiti

Founded in 1855 at East Grinstead, Sussex, England, the Society soon established affiliated houses in Aberdeen, London and Boston, USA (1873). The sisters came to Haiti from Boston in 1927. The recitation of the Divine Office and the daily Eucharist are central to the life of the sisters who have a particular devotion to the Holy Name as well as to serving God in the poor.

Habit: Light grey habit and veil with white rim and collar, SSM cross
Membership: 6
Superior: Sister Marjorie Raphael, SSM

Holy Trinity School, Box 857, Port-au-Prince, Haiti
St. Vincent's School for the Handicapped, Box 1319, Port-au-Prince, Haiti
Foyer Notre Dame, Box 857, Port-au-Prince, Haiti
Maison St. Paul, Box 857, Port-au-Prince, Haiti
Mailing addresses for all of the above, sent from outside of Haiti: Name of Institution (adding "P-au-P"), Agape Flats, 7990 15th Street East, Sarasota, FL 34243, USA
See also England, Scotland, Sri Lanka, and USA.

INDIA (Church of North India)

Christa Prema Siva Ashram
Mixed
B

Shivajinagal
Pure 411005
India

Founded as an Anglican ashram in 1927, it was re-established as an ecumenical community in 1972. The foundation members were from the Community of St. Mary the Virgin, Wantage, and the Roman Catholic Society of the Sacred Heart of Jesus. A Hindu woman also formed part of the original group; however she has since died. Guests are welcome to join in the simple life of the community and share in the Indian liturgy. Instruction on meditation and Indian or Christian spirituality is given on request.

Habit: Members already belonging to a religious order
continue to do so and wear their community cross;
otherwise no habit is worn except Indian dress.
Membership: 6
Leader: The Acharya

IRELAND

Society of St. Francis
Men
RV   B   C

St. Francis House
75 Deerpark Road
Belfast BT14 7PW
Ireland
Tel: 0232 351480

A community dedicated to prayer, study and Franciscan works of mercy. Retreats, parish work, and mission work.

Habit: Brown habit with capuce, white rope
Membership: 4
Guardian: Br. Hubert, SSF

See also Australia, England, USA, New Zealand, Scotland, Papua New Guinea and Solomon Islands.

JAPAN

Community of Nazareth
Women

16-41 Shirokane
6 Chome
Minatoku
Tokyo
108 Japan

Branch houses at Sendai and Okinawa.

JERUSALEM AND THE MIDDLE EAST

Community of Emmanuel Sisters and Brothers
Mixed

Evangelical Home for Girls
PO Box 142
Ramallah
via Israel

The community was founded in 1968 and is committed to a life of prayer and living by faith, working the ministry of home and school. It consists of regular sisters who are celibate and members of the Emmanuel Fellowship who pray for the work in Ramallah and at Emmanuel House in Swansea, Wales, UK.

Habit: Small silver cross inscribed with "Emmanuel"
Membership: 7
Superior: Sr. Verena Wittwer

See also Wales.

KOREA

Society of the Holy Cross
Women
RV   B

Holy Cross Convent
3 Chong-dong
Chung-ku
Seoul
Korea

The society was founded in Seoul in 1925 and, until
World War II, received support from the Community of St.
Peter, England.   It was engaged in evangelistic and
parochial work until the 1970's when they became active
in social welfare and education work. The retreat house
program involves Bible studies, vocational counselling,
prayer meetings and quiet days.

Habit: Traditional black with girdle and white wimple
    with cross
Membership: 20
Superior: The Rev'd Mother Catherine, SHC

Bona's House, Naeamni, Kadok-myon, Chongwon-kun 363-
850, Korea
St. Anne's House, 619-28 Onsuri, Kilsang-myon, Kanghwa-
kun 417-840, Korea
St. Peter's School, 1 Hang-dong, Kuro-ku, Seoul 152-140,
Korea

Jesus Abbey
Mixed

Box 17
Taebaek
Kangwondo 235-600
Republic of Korea

Jesus Abbey, situated in the Diocese of Taejon, is a base for evangelising. It aims to provide a lay training and study centre from which missionary teams can be sent out with a vision based upon a new pattern of church life. The key to the vision is community life discovered in "becoming part of a supernatural family in Christ." While the membership is presently made up of Anglicans, it aims to be ecumenical and it describes its spirituality as a modified form of the Benedictine tradition. Celibacy is optional.

Habit: A simple wooden cross with stigmata symbol
Membership: 22
Superior: The Rev'd Jeremiah Chu

Sisters of St. Francis
Women
RV B

Chung cheong bukdo Chopieong myen
Yeong jengri 483-12
South Korea

Established in 1988, the order did pastoral work and medical work in the leprosy village of the Seoul Diocese. After receiving diocesan recognition in the following year the sisters have become involved in parish work. The sisters want to be like our Lord Jesus Christ through the model of St. Francis and work with the poor and alienated.

Habit: Habit with white collar, veil and insignia

Membership: 3
Superior: Sr. Theresa Ok Nam Som, SOF

MALAYSIA

Community of the Good Shepherd
Women
RV   B

PO Box No.17
91007 Sandakan
Sabah
Malaysia

The community of the Good Shepherd is a teaching order which unites its work in education and the parish to a life of prayer.

Habit: White cassock with silver COGS cross
Membership: 2
Superior: Sr. Oi Chin

MOZAMBIQUE

Sisters of St. Paul
Women
RV

Maputo
Mozambique

The Sisters of St. Paul, Mozambique's own indigenous order of nuns, was born in the middle of violence, to help deal with it. They work with the street boys, orphaned through attacks of the surrounding villages. The boys then make their way to Maputo and live by stealing. They have 22 of them sleeping in one room of the little convent; others sleep outside on the lorry to stop its being stolen.

NEW ZEALAND

Society of the Holy Cross
Men

56 Reeves Road
Pakuranga
Auckland
New Zealand
Tel: 09 566 325

Better known by its Latin initials SSC—the *Society Sanctae Crucis*.   Membership is open to priests who sanctify the priestly life by rule, unite members in a special bond of charity, faith, and discipline, extend catholic principles and strive for corporate reunion with the Roman Catholic Church.

Provincial Vicar: The Rev'd H.V. Leigh, SSC

See also England and USA.

Community of the Sacred Name
Women
RV   B   C

181 Barbadoes Street
Christchurch 1
New Zealand

Founded in 1893 with the help of the Community of St. Andrew, London, the sisters are engaged in providing retreats and quiet days. Branch houses were established in Fiji, in the Diocese of Polynesia, and in the Wellington diocese where sisters have undertaken city mission work and chaplaincy duties at the university.

Habit: Black habit with scapular, girdle and veil, silver cross on oak medallion; pale blue or white habits worn in summer and in Fiji

Membership: 22
Superior: The Rev'd Mother, CSN

40 Rintoul Street, Wellington, New Zealand
See also Fiji.

Community of St. Francis
Women
RV   B   C

St. Francis House
33 Carlton Gore Road
Grafton
Auckland 1
New Zealand
Tel: 09 798 869

Founded from England in 1986, the sisters are linked with the European province of CSF for support. They are part of the First Order of the Society of St. Francis and are engaged in mission, parish and pastoral work and social action.

Habit: Brown habit with white collar and rope, no veil
Membership: 6
Minister Provincial: Sister Teresa, CSF

See also England and USA.

Society of St. Francis
Men
RV   B   C

St. Francis Friary
1A Brighton Road
Parnell
Auckland 1
PO Box 37-014

New Zealand
Tel: 09 771 292

A community dedicated to prayer, study and Franciscan works of mercy. Retreats, parish work and mission work.

Habit: Brown habit with capuce, white rope

See also Australia, Belize, England, Ireland, Scotland, Papua New Guinea, Solomon Islands, and USA.

PAPUA NEW GUINEA

Melanesian Brotherhood
Men
B

PO Box 21
Pomete
Kandrian
West New Britain Province
Papua New Guinea

Founded in 1926 the Brotherhood worked in areas where the gospel had not been preached and with lapsed Christians. The brothers work on parish missions and with the local church. The Brotherhood do not take life vows but are professed for a certain period.

Habit: Medal and white-black line sash with shirt or calico
Membership: 230
Regional Brother: Br. Alphaeus Tubyiara, MBH

See also Australia and Solomon Islands.

Society of St. Francis
Men
RV   B

St. Mary of the Angels Friary
PO Box 78 Haruro
Popondetta
Papua New Guinea

The Franciscans undertake medical care, mission and parish work, and work in education. As part of the worldwide Society of St. Francis, the friars in Papua New Guinea use the Franciscan Office Book belonging to the European province of the Society for their daily liturgy.

Habit: Cross and brown shirt
Membership: Not known
Guardian: Br. Timothy Joseph, SSF

St. Maximillian's Friary, PO Box 26, Popondetta, Northern Province, Papua New Guinea
Douglas House, PO Box 3411, Lae, Morobe Province, Papua New Guinea
See also Australia, Belize, England, Ireland, New Zealand, Scotland, Solomon Islands, and USA.

Community of the Visitation
Women

Hetune
Nr Popendatta
Northern Province
Papua New Guinea

PHILIPPINES

Order of St. Anne
Women
RV   B

251 Sinsuat Avenue
Cotabato City
Philippines

Founded in the United States in 1910, the sisters live a modified Benedictine Rule dedicated to a life of prayer, mission and good works.

Habit: White veil, gray scapular and dress, black girdle and ebony cross with white trim
Superior: Sr. Anna Clara, OSA

See also USA.

Sisters of St. Mary the Virgin
Women
RV   B

Convent of Sisters of St. Mary the Virgin
Sagada
Mt. Prov.
Philippines

An indigenous order engaged in a variety of good works including social welfare, education, parish and retreat work. Membership of the community is extended to associates and friends..

Habit: White veil, blue dress and scapular, with black girdle and cross with SSMV
Membership: 5
Superior: The Rev'd Mother Clare, SSMV

Holy Angels Convent, Pico, La Tinidad, Benguet, Philippines

PUERTO RICO

Order of St. Benedict
Mixed
MV   B

Order of St. John the Baptist and St. Benedict
Street 2 #159, Saint Just

Trujillo Alto,
Puerto Rico 00978

Founded in 1985, the community live under the Benedictine Rule, looking to the greater glory of God and the sanctification of lives in the Easter joy of the Risen Lord. The work of the order is varied, including hospitality, retreats, education and evangelisation. In addition to the Liturgy of the Eucharist the community recite a four-fold office.

Habit: White tunic and scapular with belt
Membership: 18
Abbot: The Rt. Rev'd Alberto Morales OSB

Novitiate—The Reconciliation Priory, HC-08 #175, Ponce, Puerto Rico 00731-9703

SCOTLAND

Order of the Holy Paraclete
Women
RV   B   C

Scottish Churches' House
The Mosset
Kirk Street
Dunblane
Perthshire
FK15 0AJ
Scotland

A branch house of the sisters at Sneaton Castle, Whitby. Active work combined with a monastic structure to the daily life. The rule is modern but basically Benedictine in emphasis.   For further details please see OHP Whitby (England).

Habit: Grey with black cincture and veil
Membership: 3

Superior: Sr. Janet, OHP

See also England, Ghana and South Africa.

Society of Our Lady of the Isles
Mixed

Our Lady of the Isles
Isle of Feltar
Shetland
Scotland
Tel: 0957 83 200

Society of St. Francis
Men
RV   B   C

Little Portion
111/2 Lothian Road
Edinburgh
EH3 9AN
Scotland
Tel: 031 228 3077

A community dedicated to prayer, study and Franciscan works of mercy. Retreats, parish work and mission work.

Habit: Brown habit with capuche, white rope

1/1, 144 Stamford Street, Barrowfield, Glasgow G31 4AU
See also Australia, Belize, England, Ireland, New Zealand, Papua New Guinea, Solomon Islands and USA.

Society of St. Margaret—Scotland
Women
RV   B   C

Convent of St. Margaret of Scotland
17 Spital
Aberdeen

Scotland
AB2 3HT
Tel: 0224 632648

Founded in 1864 as an autonomous off-shoot of the Society of St. Margaret at East Grinstead, the convent was in fact the first daughter house to be set up by a religious community (and to be granted immediate independence) since the dissolution of the monastic houses at the Reformation three hundred years before. The sisters are engaged in retreat work, especially the provision of private retreats, and run a home for the elderly in the convent grounds.

Habit: Grey habit with scapular and black girdle and veil, SSM black cross with white inset
Membership: 3
Superior: The Rev'd Mother Verity, SSM

See also England, Haiti, Sri Lanka, and USA.

Community of the Transfiguration
Mixed
MV C

Monastery of the Transfiguration
23 Manse Road
Roslin
Midlothian
EH25 9LF
Scotland

Founded in 1965 with the support of the Bishop of Edinburgh and the Roman Catholic Abbot of Nunraw, the community is ecumenical. The Community is called to a life of prayer and solitude; and vows are made according to the Cistercian rite. They are engaged in work with the poor and destitute.

Habit: Charcoal grey flannel habit with leather belt
Membership: 4
Superiors: The Rev'd Br. John Halsey, CT
　　　　　　The Rev'd Sr. P. Burgess

Independent house for sisters: 70E Clerk Street, Loanhead, Midlothian

SEYCHELLES

Community of the Sacred Passion
Women

Victoria
Seychelles
Indian Ocean

SOLOMON ISLANDS

Melanesian Brotherhood
Men
B

PO Box 19
Tabalia
Guadalcanal
Solomon Islands

Founded in 1926, the Brotherhood worked in areas where the gospel had not been preached and with lapsed Christians. The Brotherhood do not take life vows but are professed for a certain period of time.

Habit: Medal and white-black line sash with shirt or calico
Membership: 230
Superior: The Regional Brother

See also Australia and Papua New Guinea.

73

Society of St. Francis
Men
RV   B

La Verna Friary
Hautambu
PO Box 519 Honiara
Solomon Islands

The presence of Franciscans in the Solomon Islands began in 1970. The brothers are part of the Pacific Islands province of the Society and are engaged in mission, parish and social work.

Habit: Franciscan habit (see SSF England) or brown
    shirt and SSF cross
Membership: 35
Assistant Minister: Brother Giles, SSF

Patteson House, PO Box 519, Honiara, Solomon Islands
Canon Usumae Friary, Kira Kira, Makira Ulawa Province,
Solomon Islands
The Friary, PO Box 7, Auki, Malaita Province, Solomon
Islands
See also Australia, Belize, England, Ireland, New Zealand,
Papua New Guinea, Scotland, and USA.

Community of the Sisters of the Church
RV   B

Tetete ni Kolivuti
Box 510
Honiara
Solomon Islands

The first sisters, sent by the mother house in Richmond, England, arrived in Honiara in 1970. The sisters now teach in kindergartens and primary schools as well as undertaking pastoral work, parish work and leading retreats. Mingling adoration and action the sisters try to promote the honour and glory of God and the extension of his kingdom upon earth.

Habit: Grey veil with blue trim and skirt, CSC cross
Membership: 13
Superior: Sister Lilian Maiva, CSC

Patteson House, Box 510, Honiara, Solomon Islands
Sisters of the Church, Fo'au Village, Malaita, Solomon Islands
St. Gabriels's, Aola Village, PO Box 19, Tabalia, Guadalcanal, Solomon Islands
See also Australia, Canada and England.

SOUTH AFRICA

Oratory of the Good Shepherd
Men
C

The Deanery
PO Box 207
Eshowe, 3815
Republic of South Africa
Tel: 0354 41726/41215

The Oratory is a society of celibate priests and laymen of the Anglican Communion who are endeavouring under the direction of a rule, to live a life of devotion and service. At present there are members working in Cape Town, Pretoria and Zululand.

See also England and USA.

Community of the Holy Name
Women
RV   B   C

Convent of the Holy Name
PO Box 43
Lesotho 300
Lesotho
Republic of South Africa
Tel: 050 40249

Founded in 1962 from CHN England, the sisters maintain a life of prayer, recite a daily five-fold office and attend Mass daily. Each house has a garden in which the sisters grow some of their own food. The community at Lesotho also has its own wafer baking department, church needlework department and another group who make Mothers' Union uniforms. Some of the sisters are also involved with youth work, prison visiting, pastoral work and further education.

Habit: Grey habit with grey or black veil and crucifix, white collar
Superior: Sister Alphoncina, CHN

PO Box 87, Maseru, Lesotho, Republic of South Africa, Tel: 050 322524
St. Stephen's Mission, PO Box 22, Mohales Hoek 800, Lesotho, Republic of South Africa, Tel: 050 85328 Parish work
St. Luke's Mission, Maphophoma, PO Box 175, Nongoma, 3950, Kwazulu Works: parish work, homecraft group, garden & poultry
Isandlwana Mission, PO Box 2045, Dundee, 3000 Children's home
Convent of the Holy Name, Kwamagwaza, PB 806, Melmoth, 3835, Tel: 03545 2892
Convent of the Holy Name, PO Box 175, Nongoma 3950
Convent of the Holy Name, PO Box 675, Nqutu 3135 Novitiate, pastoral work and provincial house
See also England.

Order of the Holy Paraclete
Women
RV B   C

St. Benedict's House
PO Box 49027
Rosettenville 2130
Transvaal
Republic of South Africa
Tel: (011) 26-2958

St. Benedict's House was founded in 1957 by the order, which is based in Whitby, England. It is a retreat and conference centre which can accommodate 20 people. The sisters live under a modern rule inspired by St. Benedict which allows for an active apostolate with a strong contemplative base. The confraternity includes tertiaries, friends and associates.

Habit: Grey habit with white collar, black veil and girdle, OHP cross
Membership: 4
Superior: The Sister-in-charge

P.O. Box 1272, Manzini, South Africa
See also England, Ghana, and Scotland.

Society of the Precious Blood
Women
RV   B   C

Priory of Our Lady Mother of Mercy
Masite Mission
PO Box 7192
Maseru
Lesotho
Republic of South Afrcia

77

Founded in 1957 by some sisters from Burnham Abbey (Society of Precious Blood, England), the sisters form a multi-racial contemplative community joining with a group of Basuto women. The Masite branch of SPB became autonomous in 1966 and is now different in many respects, although the sisters keep the same spiritual rule and constitutions. The sisters are dedicated to intercession and keep a watch, or chain of prayer, before the Blessed Sacrament all day. In their life they try to witness against the evil of apartheid and give reality to their prayer for justice and reconciliation.

Habit: Black tunic and veil with red cord for cross, and red girdle
Membership: 12
Prioress: The Rev'd Mother Prioress, SPB

The Sister's House, 46 Green Street, West End, Kimberley 8301, Cape Province, South Africa
See also England.

Community of the Resurrection
Men
RV   B   C

St. Peter's Priory
PO Box 991 Southdale
2135
Republic of South Africa
Tel: 011 434-2504

The community was founded in 1892. Since 1898 the mother house had been at Mirfield in West Yorkshire, England. A priory was established in Johannesburg in 1903 to minister primarily to African Anglicans in the Transvaal. Parishes and schools were created along with St. Peter's College for training parish priests. The community works for justice and unity and for a deeper commitment to Christ. For further information please see the entry for CR Mirfield, England.

Habit: Winter: black sarum cassock, leather belt and grey scapular; summer: white cassock, leather belt and black scapular;CR cross attached to belt by chain

Membership: 6

Superior: The Rev'd the Provincial, CR

PO Box 49027, Rossettenville, 2130, South Africa
See also England.

Community of the Resurrection of Our Lord
Women
RV   B   C

PO Box 72
Grahamstown 6140
Republic of South Africa
Tel: 0461 22701

Founded in 1884 by the fourth bishop of Grahamstown. The sisters are engaged in chaplaincy work and cater for retreats, quiet days and conferences.

Superior: The Rev'd Mother Superior, CR

See also England.

Society of the Sacred Mission
Men
RV   B

St. Augustine's Priory
Modderpoort Estate
PO Modderpoort
9746
Republic of South Africa
Tel: Ladybrand 3140

Founded in England in 1893, the society are engaged in educational, pastoral,and missionary work.

Habit: Black cassock, capuce with hood, and red girdle
    with crucifix
Membership: 5
Superior: The Rev'd Fr. Andrew Longley, SSM

PO Box 1579, Maseru 100, Republic of South Africa, Tel:
Maseru 315979
See also Australia and England.

Community of St. John the Baptist
Women
RV   B   C

PO St. Cuthbert's
Transkei
Republic of South Africa

Works: Weaving school, care of St. Margaret's Hostel for Girls, Sunday schools, guides, visiting, church sewing, running the diocesan retreat and conference centre.

Society of St. John the Divine
Women
RV   B   C

Convent of St. John the Divine
PO Box 12183
Jacobs 4026, Natal
Republic of South Africa

Founded in 1887, the society were originally involved with schools and institutions. The sisters were engaged in parish work in the Durban area, working among Indian and Coloureds and latterly with Whites as well. The society have now withdrawn from active parish work and are more involved with diocesan work, occasional preaching and retreat work. The sisters also distribute second hand clothing and food to those in need.

Habit: White dress with black scapular and veil, white V-shaped collar and black girdle with profession crucifix
Membership: 8
Superior: The Rev'd Mother Mary Evelyn, SSJD

Community of St. Mary the Virgin
Women
RV   B   C

Irene Homes
PO Irene, 1675
Republic of South Africa
Tel: 012 667-1035/667-2032

The first CSMV sisters came to South Africa in 1903 to take charge of St. Mary's Diocesan School, Pretoria, a work which continued until 1975. In 1904 a House of Mercy opened in Pretoria and later moved to Irene. Today the Irene Homes is a diocesan institution caring for the mentally handicapped and a few old people. The sisters live in the grounds in a new convent dedicated to "St. Mary at the Cross." While there is a South African novitiate now, most of the novices have chosen to complete their training at Wantage, the mother house. In recent years there has been a big increase in the numbers of oblates who commit themselves to prayer in fellowship with the sisters and keep a rule of life.

Habit: Blue dress and veil, with white cap and collar
Membership: 12
Provincial Superior: The Rev'd Mother Muriel Grace, CSMV

See also England.

Community of St. Michael and All Angels
Women
RV   B   C

St. Michael's House
PO Box 79
9300 Bloemfontein
Republic of South Africa
Tel: 051 473805/471160

Founded in 1874, in order to undertake immense pioneer works, nursing, education for white and black children, and mission, it was originally referred to as a diocesan sisterhood. It was the first religious community to be established in the province. The sisters are now engaged in a variety of active work and live on the campus of St. Michael's School, now government-run.

Habit: Blue habit with white veil and copper cross
Membership: 8
Superior: The Rev'd Mother Doreen Mary, CSM&AA

SPAIN

Fraternidad Ecumenica Franciscana
Mixed
B

Calle Santa Clara, 5
41002 Sevilla
Spain

Founded in 1991 as part of the Third Order of the Franciscans, the Franciscan Ecumenical Fraternity commit themselves to preaching the gospel and declaring Jesus as Saviour. Working with the unemployed, the marginalized and the poor they provide hot food to those in need. They also meet for healing services and talks on Franciscan spirituality.

SRI LANKA (CEYLON)

Society of St. Margaret
Women
RV   B

St. Margaret's Convent
157 St. Michael's Road
Polwatte
Colombo 3
Sri Lanka

Three English sisters arrived in Sri Lanka in 1887 from St. Margaret's East Grinstead. Now the sisters working in Colombo and Moratuwa are all Sri Lankan. They run children's homes, work for young people, the very poor and the elderly. As with SSM in England the sisters also take a vow of charity along with the usual three religious vows.

Habit: White habit with scapular, SSM ebony cross, and
    black veil
Membership: 9
Superior: Sister Lucy Agnes, SSM

St. John's Home, Moratuwa, Sri Lanka
See also England, Haiti, Scotland, and USA.

TANZANIA

Chama Cha Fransisi
Mixed

Mtakatifu
Mtandi
Tanzania

Founded in 1987.

Community of St. Mary of Nazareth and Calvary
Women
RV B

Community of St. Mary
Kilimani Masasi
PO Box 502
Masasi
Mtwara Region
Tanzania

The community was founded in 1946 with the help of the first Bishop of Masasi. They aim to serve God by identifying wholly with his will and by their lives of service with his people. The sisters' life is centred around the daily Mass and offices. The community work in order to be self-supporting. Today there are seven branch houses receiving women from every diocese in the Church of the Province of Tanzania.

Habit: Blue habit and girdle with white collar and veil, CMM cross
Membership: 90
Superior: The Rev'd Mother Magdalene, CMM

Newala, PO Box 116, Newala-Mtwara, Tanzania
Mtwara, Box 162, Mtwara, Tanzania
DSM, PO Box 25016, Dar-es-Salaam
PO Box 35, Korogwe, Tanga Region, Tanzania
Njombe, PO Box 150, Njombe, Iringa Region, Tanzania
Liuli, PO Box 6, Liuli, Mbinga, Ruvuma Region
Kwa Mkono, PO Box Kwa Mkono Handeni, Tanga, Tanzania
PO Box 45, Tanga, Tanzania

UNITED STATES OF AMERICA

All Saints Sisters of the Poor
Women
RV B C

All Saints Convent
PO Box 3127
Catonsville, MD 21228-0127
USA

The order was founded in London in 1851, and the American congregation became autonomous in 1890. The rule does not enjoin any particular type of service. The work that has developed is one of hospitality—guests, counselling, quiet days, retreats etc. The sisters are Augustinian and emphasize prayer and liturgical worship, trying to realize the special value of the evangelical counsels (vows) in this age.

Habit: Black habit with scapular, traditional Augustinian black veil and white wimple, plain wooden cross on girdle

Membership: 20

Superior: The Rev'd Mother Catherine Grace of All Saints

Jos Richey House, 828 North Eutaw, Baltimore MD 21201, USA Hospice for patients with terminal illness run in conjunction with Mount Calvary Church, Baltimore, Maryland
St. Anna's Residence, 2016 Race, Philadelphia, PA 19103, USA, Tel: (215) 567-2943 Residential hostel for women and students opened in 1913
St. Gabriel's Retreat House, PO Box 3106, Catonsville, MD 21228-0106, Tel: (301) 747-6767
See Society of All Saints, England.

Order of the Ascension
Mixed
MV

1042 Preston Avenue
Charlottesville, VA 22903
USA
Tel: (804) 293-3157

A community of priests under vows, serving parishes that are poor, working class, urban minority, isolated, small or historically unstable. The Order maintains a common life under rule of yearly retreat, continuing education and vacation. Corporate ministries include Ascension Press and the Parish Development Institute.

Contact: The Rev'd Fr. Scott A. Benhase

Sisters of Charity
Women
RV   B

Wellspring Retreat House and Convent
PO Box 818
701 Park Place
Boulder City, NV 89005
USA
Tel: (702) 293-4988

The Community was founded in Bristol, England, in 1869 and uses the rule given by St. Vincent de Paul to the first Sisters of Charity in France in the seventeenth century. The work in America began in 1967. In 1981 the convent and retreat center was opened, dedicated to the Holy Spirit and is a spiritual oasis in the Nevada desert. The sisters undertake mission and evangelistic work, prison ministry and nursing, home visiting and counselling.

Habit: Navy blue jacket and skirt, white blouse and navy
     veil, SC cross
Membership: 28
Superior: Sister Faith Mary, SC

See also England and Wales.

Community of Christian Family Ministry
Mixed

801 Valley Crest Drive
Vista, CA 92084
USA
Tel: (619) 727-1848

Composed of laity and clergy, men and women, single and married, catholic and charismatic as well as evangelical. Ministry extends to hospital visitation, preaching, retreats, counselling, drama, and music. Oblates, companions and associates share the same rule.

Co-ordinators: Dennis and Elizabeth Kelly

Congregation of the Companions of the Holy Saviour
Men
RV   B   C

56 Holyoke Street
Brewer, ME 04412-1906
USA

Founded in 1891 by a group of priests desiring to live under a rule of celibacy and a common discipline of devotion and study. Only priests, deacons and candidates for holy orders are eligible for membership, although laity and clergy may become associates. At the present time all the companions are parochial clergy, so there is no central house. Monthly conferences, annual chapter and retreat.

Habit: Black cassock, grey scapular and pewter cross
Membership: 7
Master: The Rev'd Ian Bockus, CCHS

Oratory of the Good Shepherd
Men
RV   B   C

The American College, OGS
Box 16226
Baltimore, MD 21210
USA

Founded in 1913 as a secular institute for priests and non-ordained brothers. Oratorians live a common rule which requires celibacy, daily offices, daily Eucharist, and a pattern of study. While a common life is encouraged, it is not required. OGS has a strong tradition of scholarship, pastoral work and spiritual direction.

Habit: Black cassock, scapular and OGS lapel cross
Prior: The Rev'd Martin Davidson, OGS

See also England and South Africa.

Hie Hill Community
Mixed
C   B

The Hie Hill Center
26 Chittendon Hill Road
Westbrook, CT 06498
USA

A non-residential community, lay and ordained, who seek to live out their baptismal covenant in the light of the Benedictine tradition. They focus on conservation, manual labour, and hospitality.

Contact: The Presiding Officer

Order of the Holy Cross
Men
MV   B   C

Mount Calvary
PO 1296
Santa Barbara, CA 94709

USA
Tel: (805) 963-8175

A monastic and apostolic community founded in 1884 in New York. In 1987 the community changed the three-fold expression of religious vows to the traditional Benedictine vows. The corporate offering of the Eucharist and four-fold Divine Office is central to the order. The brethren are engaged in teaching, preaching, counselling, direction, parish ministry and community service. To this end the order have urban houses, from which members go out to work in the local community, as well as traditional monasteries. The confraternity includes a celibate society for priests, oblates, associates and friends. Mount Calvary Retreat House offers individual and group retreats, conferences, etc.

Habit: White tunic and scapular with hood and plain
    black cross
Membership: 45
Superior: The Rev'd Br. William Sibley, OHC

Holy Cross Monastery, PO Box 99, West Park, NY 12493, Tel: (914) 384-6660 Est. 1904 Located on Hudson River, offering retreats and study programs.
Incarnation Priory, 1601 Oxford Street, Berkeley, CA 94709, Tel: (415) 548-3406 Est. 1972 as an ecumenical community shared by OHC and the Roman Catholic Camaldolese Benedictines. Providing house of studies for both orders and some limited guest accommodation.
Absalom Jones Priory, 455 West 148th Street, New York, NY 10031, Tel: (212) 926-1400 Est. 1973 enabling monks to undertake a variety of works in Harlem and to provide local parishes with assistance.
Mount Calvary Retreat House and Novitiate, PO Box 1296, Santa Barbara, CA 93102
See also Canada and Ghana.

Society of the Holy Cross
Men

130 East 4th
Mt. Carmel, IL 62863
USA

Better known by its Latin initials SSC, the Society is the oldest catholic society in the Anglican Communion. A secular institute open to priests and bishops to sanctify the priestly life by rule, uniting members in a special bond of charity, faith, discipline etc. It aims to extend catholic principles, and strive for corporate reunion with Rome.

Provincial Vicar: The Rev'd J.F.T. Oates

See also England and New Zealand.

Order of the Holy Family
Mixed
40 Charleston Road
Willingboro, NJ 08046
USA
Tel: (609) 877-2354

The rule is inspired by the Celtic tradition, and includes the adoration of God, reverence for creation, hospitality and creative work. The Order includes oblates and associates.

Abbot: The Rt. Rev'd Jon Aidan

Sisterhood of the Holy Nativity
Women
RV   B   C

101 E. Division St.
Fond du Lac, WI 54935
USA
Tel: (414) 921-2560

Founded in 1882, SHN was the first Anglican religious group to undertake missionary work with Native Americans, having established a mission house on the Oneida Indian Reservation. Currently, the community is involved in areas of pastoral care—providing retreats, quiet days and missions to parishes etc. The sisterhood is loyal to the traditional Anglican faith and practice and considers prayer its primary work.

Habit: Black tunic with scapular, veil with white rim and white collar, SHN cross with symbol of Incarnation

Membership; 17

Superior: The Rev'd Mother Boniface, SHN

St. Mary's Retreat House, 505 E. Los Olivos, Santa Barbara, CA 93105, USA, Tel: (805) 682-4117

7310 Old Harbor Avenue, Anchorage, AK 99504, USA

Order of the Holy Redeemer
Mixed
RV   B   C

Holy Redeemer Abbey
14 Kennedy Way
Keansburg, NJ 07734
USA

The Redemptorists are devoted to mission to the poor, the disenfranchised, the neglected and the unchurched in society. Members are engaged in evangelism, Christian education programs, feeding the hungry and social work. The rule is designed to meet the needs of everyday life. Daily offices are from the BCP. Vows of simplicity, chastity and obedience are made. Oblates and associates share in the order's ministry, which is parish centered.

Habit: Tunic, scapular, girdle and capuche, crucifix ring and OHR cross

Membership: 52
Abbot: The Rt. Rev'd Charles William, OHR

Community of the Holy Spirit
Women
RV   B   C

St. Hilda's House
621 West 113 Street
New York, NY   10025
USA
Tel: (212) 666-8249

Living under the Rule of St. Augustine, the sisters' life is centered on liturgical prayer. They are engaged in chaplaincy work, spiritual direction and work in the field of Christian education.

Superior: The Rev'd Mother Madelaine Mary, CHS

St. Hilda's & St. Hugh's School, 619 West 114 Street, New York, NY 10025, USA
Melrose School, St. Cuthbert's Retreat & Conference Center, RD 5, Federal Hill Rd., Brewster, NY 10509, USA, Tel: (914) 279-2406

Order of Julian of Norwich
Mixed

600 21st
Racine, WI 53403
USA
Tel: (414) 633-1650

A traditionally monastic, semi-enclosed, contemplative community which follows the spirituality of Dame Julian of Norwich. There are associate and oblate affiliations for laity and clergy.

Guardian: The Rev'd Fr. John-Julian, OJN

S10 W26392 Summit Avenue, Waukesha, WI 53188, USA
Tel: (414) 549-0452

Life in Jesus Community
Mixed
C

Box 40
Libertytown, MD 21762
USA

A covenant community for clergy and lay men and women, married or celibate. Ecumenical in outreach, the community is committed to a ministry of evangelism, church renewal and healing. Members follow a simple rule.

Rector: The Rev'd Philip C. Zampino

Company of the Paraclete
Mixed

61 Erie
Jersey City
NJ 07302
USA

A modern, ecumenical order, both communal and solitary, which is dedicated as devotion to the Holy Spirit to helping the poor help themselves. The company follow a Franciscan spirituality.

Contact: Br. Thomas

Box 61399, Seattle, WA 98121

Poor Clares of the Reparation
Women
RV   B

St. Clare's Convent
PO Box 342
Mt. Sinai, NY 11766
USA
Tel: (516) 473-0659

The order of PCR is a semi-cloistered contemplative community of women devoted to the life and work of prayer. It was founded in 1922 under the spiritual direction of the Franciscans; and is now the Second Order of the Society of St. Francis, American Province.

Habit: Brown tunic, white collar and cord, black veil with white band on cap
Membership: 3
Superior: Sister Mary Philomena, PCR

Order of St. Anne
Women
RV B C

Bethany House
Box No 1373
17 Claremont Avenue
East Arlington, MA 02174-0022
USA
Tel: (617) 643-0921

The Bethany sisters recently moved from Lincoln, after a period of discerning what new ministries God was calling them to. Founded in 1910, the order now comprises several autonomous houses listed below.

Habit: Light grey, white collar and black veil with white rim, OSA cross
Membership: 20
Superior: The Rev'd Mother Maria Dolorosa, OSA

St. Anne's House, 15 Craigie St, Cambridge, MA 02138, USA
Convent of St. Anne, 1125 N. LaSalle St, Chicago, IL 60610 USA
Convent of St. Anne, 18 Claremont Avenue, Arlington, MA 02174, USA
See also the Philippines.

Order of St. Benedict
Men
B

Chicago Priory of Christ the King
#110, 4334 N. Hazel Street
Chicago, IL 60613
USA

The brothers began their ministry through Christ the King in 1985, and are located by the inner city Chicago neighborhood of Uptown. They are called to a Benedictine life encompassing both prayer and service, and are active participants in the parish life of the Church of the Atonement. The Brothers publish biblical study guides for the Gospel text used in the lectionary cycle, which are suitable for either individuals or parish Bible study groups. They also minister to poor and newly immigrant people with a strong emphasis on biblical discipleship.

Habit: Black Cassinese Benedictine habit, with grey cincture.
Membership: Two solemnly professed brothers, and resident oblates.
Contact: Br. Ned Gerber, OSB

Order of St. Benedict—St. Gregory's Abbey
Men
MV   B   C

St. Gregory's Abbey
56500 Abbey Road
Three Rivers, MI 49093-9595
Tel: (616) 244-5893

Established in 1939 at Valparaiso, Indiana, and moving to Three Rivers in 1949, the community was for 30 years a dependence of Nashdom Abbey in England. In 1969 it became an independent Abbey. The community are contemplative Benedictines engaging in work, study and prayer. The center of their day is the conventual Eucharist in its setting of the seven-fold Divine Office. Occasional parish work is undertaken as well as private or group retreats at the monastery.

Habit: Black tunic and scapular with hood
Membership: 10
Abbot: The Rt. Rev'd Dom Andrew Marr, OSB

Order of St. Benedict—Servants of Christ
Men
MV   B

28 West Pasadena Ave
Phoenix, AZ 85013-2002
USA
Tel: (602) 248-9321

Founded in 1968 as the Servants of Christ under a modified Benedictine Rule, the community adopted the Rule of St. Benedict and the Benedictine habit three years ago. They celebrate a daily Mass and four-fold Divine Office and strive to keep a balance of worship, study and work. Their monastic witness is in an urban setting where a number of oblates meet with the community on a regular basis.

Habit: Black tunic and scapular with hood

Membership: 2
Prior: The Very Rev'd Dom Cornelius deRijk, OSB

Community of St. Francis
Women
RV   B   C

St. Francis House
502 Pawnee Street
Bethlehem, PA 18015
USA
Tel: (215) 691-7973

Franciscan sisters living a life of prayer, study and apostolic work with special concern for the poor and deprived. Confraternity includes associates and tertiaries.

Habit: Simple long brown dress, knotted rope, no veil
Membership: 7

3743 Army Street, San Francisco, CA 94110, USA, Tel: (415) 824-0288
See also England and New Zealand.

Society of St. Francis
Men
RV   B   C

Wayside House
Box 389
Mt. Sinai, NY 11766
USA
Tel: (516) 473-9434

A community of priests and laymen dedicated to prayer, study and Franciscan works of mercy. Retreats, parochial supply and mission work.

Habit: Brown habit with capuche, white rope girdle
Provincial Minister: Br. Dominic George, SSF

Little Portion Friary, Box 399, Mt. Sinai, NY 11766, USA, Tel: (516) 473-0553
Hermitage Wayside House, Box 389, Mt. Sinai, NY 11766, USA
St. Elizabeth Friary, 1474 Bushwick Avenue, Brooklyn, NY 11207, USA, Tel: (718) 455-5963
San Damiano Friary, 573 Dolores, San Francisco, CA 94110, USA, Tel: (415) 861-1372
See also Australia, Belize, England, Ireland, New Zealand, Papua New Guina, Scotland, and Solomon Islands.

Brotherhood of St. Gregory
Men
RV   B   C

St. Bartholomew's Church
82 Prospect Street
White Plains, NY   10606
USA

Founded in 1969, the Brotherhood follow a common rule but live individually, in small groups, or with their families, supporting themselves and the community through secular or church-related work.   They strive to attain to St. Gregory's motto to be "servants of the servants of God." The rule includes the Eucharist, the four-fold office (BCP), meditation, theological study, Embertide reports, and an annual chapter.   Recognized as a Christian community, members may take life vows. Membership is also open to married men who promise poverty (support of the church), chastity (fidelity), and obedience. Brothers work in parishes as liturgists, musicians, artists, visitors to the sick, administrators, teachers and clergy.   A companion sisterhood is being encouraged.

Habit: White hooded tunic with brown scapular and
    rope; olive wood BSG cross
Membership: 28
Founder: Br. Richard Thomas Biernacki, BSG

Companion Sisterhood of St. Gregory
Women

42-27 164th
Flushing, NY 11358
USA

A Christian community-in-formation under the sponsorship of the Brotherhood of St. Gregory. Open to women, single or married, living under a common rule and serving the church on parochial, diocesan and national levels. The sisters live individually, in small groups or with their families.

Director of Vocations: Br. Christopher Stephen Jenks,
    BSG

Order of St. Helena
Women
RV   B   C

PO Box 426
Vails Gate, NY 12584
USA
Tel: (914) 562-0592

Founded in 1945, the order interprets the religious life in a modern way which enables the sisters to minister to the needs of the contemporary world. As a community the sisters are not restricted to any single area of work. The central commitment of their lives is expressed in apostolic ministry — e.g. missionary outreach, education, counselling, retreats, conferences, parish/campus work, etc.

Habit: White dress with black cross
Membership: 18
Superior: Sister Cornelia, OSH

Box 5645, Augusta, GA 30906, USA, Tel: (404) 798-5201
134 E. 28th Street, New York, NY 10016, USA, Tel: (212) 889-1124
1114 21st Avenue East, Seattle, WA 98112, USA, Tel: (206) 325-2830

Community of St. John the Baptist
Women
RV   C

Convent of St. John the Baptist
Box 240
Mendham, NJ 07945
USA
Tel: (201) 543-4641

A retreat house, parish work, retreats, workshops, Christian education, spiritual direction.

Superior: The Rev'd Mother Superior, CSJB

St. Marguerite's Retreat House, Mendham, NJ 07945, Tel: (201) 543-4582

Society of St. John the Evangelist
Men
RV   B   C

Monastery of St. Mary and St. John
980 Memorial Drive
Cambridge, MA 02138
USA
Tel: (617) 876-3037

The first religious order for men to be established in the Church of England in 1866. The Society follows a rule of life which expresses the importance of a sustained life of prayer and liturgical worship as the foundation for pastoral work and service in the context of community life. Four-fold Divine Office and Eucharist are celebrated daily. The Society operates Camp St. Augustine, a summer camp for boys aged 7-12, conducts individual retreats, spiritual direction, and Cowley Publications. Oblates, associates and friends form part of the extended community.

Habit: Black cassock and scapular with cincture with three knots, profession ring
Membership: 20
Superior: The Rev'd M. Thomas Shaw, SSJE

St. John's House, 702 W Cobb Street, Durham, NC 27707, USA, Tel: (919) 688-4161
Emery House, Emery Lane, W. Newbury, MA 01985, USA, Tel: (617) 462-7940
Camp St. Augustine (summers), 63 Mill Street, Foxborough, MA 02035, USA
See also England.

Society of St. Margaret
Women
RV   B   C

St. Margaret's Convent
17 Highland Park
Roxbury, MA 02119
USA
Tel: (617) 445-8961

Since 1855, when the Society was founded in England to minister to orphans and the sick, lives consecrated to service have been lives fulfilled. It was in 1873 that three sisters came to America to take charge of the Boston Children's Hospital and began the American House of the Society. The Society continues to work with the sick as well as in their flourishing schools.

Habit: Grey habit with scapular, black veil, belt-cincture, ebony cross with ivory cross inlaid

101

Membership: 38
Superior: The Rev'd Mother Adele Marie, SSM

PO Box 425, Boston, MA 02120, USA, Tel: (617) 523-1008
St. Margaret's House, 5419 Germantown Avenue,
Philadelphia, PA 19144, USA, Tel: (215) 844-9410
Neale House, 50 Fulton Street, New York, NY 10038, USA,
Tel: (212) 619-2672
St. Margaret's House, Jordan Road, New Hartford, NY
13413, USA, Tel: (315) 724-2324
St. Agnes House, 635 Maxwelton Court, Lexington, KY
40508, USA, Tel: (606) 254-1241 Founded in 1975 to
provide low cost housing for cancer out-patients who must
be in Lexington for treatment.
See also England, Haiti, Scotland, and Sri Lanka.

Community of St. Mary—Eastern Province
Women
RV   B   C

St. Mary's Convent
John Street
Peekskill, NY 10566
USA
Tel: (914) 737-0113

Founded in 1865 in New York City, its three provinces
became autonomous in 1985. The sisters live a semi-
enclosed monastic life centered in the daily Eucharist
and a five-fold Divine Office. Their ministry is primarily
to guests and retreatants at the convent, but sisters also
go out from time to time to speak, lead quiet days etc.
Some of the community are involved with a children's
hospital and also with their own altar bread bakery.

Habit: Dark blue habit with scapular, square white wimple
    and black veil, ebony cross with silver binding and lily
Membership: 13
Superior: The Rev'd Mother Mary Jean, CSM

Altar Bread Department, Tel: (914) 739-1289
St. Mary's Hospital for Children, 29-01 216th Street,
Bayside, NY   11360, USA, Tel: (718) 990-8800

Community of St. Mary—Southern Province
Women
RV   B   C

St. Mary's Convent
Rte 1 Box 23
Sewanee, TN 37375
USA
Tel: (615) 598-0059

Founded in 1865 in New York City, its three provinces became autonomous in 1985. The sisters run a retreat house.

Superior: The Rev'd Sister Lucy, CSM

Community of St. Mary—Western Province
Women
RV   B   C

1840 N. Prospect Ave #1040
Milwaukee, WI 53202
USA
Tel: (414) 289-0198

Founded in 1865, the Western Province was set apart in 1908 and became autonomous in 1985. The sisters live in separate apartments or in small houses in Wisconsin and are planning to re-locate at St. John's Tower. Each sister is engaged in active ministry. The ethos remains strongly Benedictine and monastic, although the sisters no longer all live in the same house.

Habit: Secular dress with the community cross—a lily embossed upon a silver cross

Membership: 9
Superior: Sister Mary Grace, CSM

St. Mary's House, 3302 N. Shepard Ave., Milwaukee, WI
53211, Tel: (414) 332-1456

Society of St. Paul
Men
RV   B   C

St. Paul the Apostle Monastery
44-660 San Pablo Avenue
Palm Desert, CA 92260
USA
Tel: (619) 568-2200

Founded in 1958, the spirituality of the society is essentially
Benedictine and is centered around private prayer, the
offices and the daily Eucharist. The community are
engaged in studies, the daily chores of the common life,
preaching, giving retreats, counselling and spiritual
direction. The monastery caters to individuals and groups.
The confraternity includes associates, friends, companions
and oblates.

Habit: Brown tunic and scapular with hood, black belt
Membership: 6
Prior: The Rev'd Fr. Barnabas Hunt, SSP

Teachers of the Children of God
Women
RV   B   C

Maycroft
Sag Harbor, NY   11963
USA
Tel: (516) 725-1121

Founded in 1934 in Rhode Island, the sisters combine their religious life with the work of teaching and furthering the work of education and religious instruction throughout the church. Franciscan by rule, the sisters are also contemplative in their spirituality, offering the seven-fold office from the monastic diurnal each day.

Habit: Full habit, all white
Membership: 10
Superior: The Rev'd Mother Virginia, TCG

Tuller School, 5870 E14th Street, Tucson, AZ 85711, USA, Tel: (602) 747-5280
Tuller School, Tuller Road, Fairfield, CT 06430, USA, Tel: (203) 374-3636

Community of the Transfiguration
Women
RV   B   C

Convent of the Transfiguration
495 Albion Avenue
Glendale, OH 45246
USA
Tel: (513) 771-5291

The community was founded in 1898 and is an active order living in the monastic tradition. The daily schedule includes time for work, meals and recreation, as well as spiritual reading, private prayer, four-fold office and the Holy Eucharist. Ministry with children and the elderly, retreats, education and recreational work.

Habit: Blue-white dress with scapular, white collar and veil, blue-white Jerusalem cross
Membership: 34
Superior: The Rev'd Mother Ann Margaret, CT

St. Monica's Recreation Center, 10022 Chester Rd.,
Cincinnati, OH 45215, USA
St. Luke's House, 322 E. McBee, Lincolnton, NC 28092,
USA
Transfiguration House, 544 4th Ferndale, Ferndale, CA
95536, USA
Bethany School, 495 Albion Avenue, Cincinnati, OH 45246,
USA
St. Mary's Memorial Home, 469 Albion Avenue, Cincinnati,
OH 45246
See also Dominican Republic.

Transfiguration Retreat
Mixed

8532 County Trunk "S"
Pulaski, WI 54162
USA

Antonian monks and nuns living a very simple semi-eremitical life, and integrating Native American spirituality.

Superior: The Prior

Community of Way of the Cross
Women

4588 South Park Avenue
Box 1945
Blasdell, NY 14219
USA
Tel: (716) 823-8877

A house of prayer, quiet, and retreat to the glory of God and the benefit of all our sisters and brothers.

Superior: The Rev'd Mother Superior

Fellowship of the Way of the Cross
Mixed

70 Highland
Holden, MA 01520
USA

A society of clergy and candidates for Holy Orders who seek to live the integration of prayer and action in ministry. The Fellowship share a rule of life and prayer. There is also an annual retreat.

Superior: The Rev'd G.P. Scruton

Worker Brothers and Sisters of the Holy Spirit
Mixed
B   C

PO Box 1704
Alamogordo, NM 88311-1704
USA

The WSHS and WBHS form an international covenant community founded in 1972 and 1979 respectively. The primary purpose of the community is to provide an opportunity for individual spiritual growth within a group which offers an experience of belonging, prayer, worship, mission, relating, discovery and commitment. Membership is open to laity and clergy regardless of marital status and is also open to teenagers. An annual retreat is held as well as monthly corporate Communions. It is Benedictine in orientation, but not lived in community. A life commitment is made to Christ, the fruit of the Spirit, mission and ministry, and members are bound by a common rule.

Habit: Smock for adults, with white rope; sweatshirt for teenagers; red for Worker sisters and grey for Worker brothers.

Membership: 170
Executive Director: Sister Meredyth James, WSHS

Central Province, 509 Margis Lane, Belton, MO 64012, USA
Northeast Province, Star Route, Box 17A, Plainfield, MA
01070, USA
Southern Province, 73 4th Arty Road, Fort Leavenworth, KS
66027, USA
See also Canada.

URUGUAY

Little Brothers and Sisters of Christ
Mixed
RV   B

St. Richard's Monastery
Cnel Juan Belinzon 4931
12000 Montevideo
Uruguay

Founded in England in 1986, the Brothers were invited
by the Bishop to establish a house in Uruguay in 1988.
Work includes hospital ancillary work and care work,
education work, and work with homeless children.

Habit: Grey with denim hood and leather belt, simple
       wooden cross
Membership: 5
Brother-in-charge: Br. Geoffrey Clement, LBC

See also England and Ghana.

WALES

Sisters of Charity
Women
RV   C

Llangasty Retreat House
Brecon

Powys
LD3 7PJ
Tel: 087 484 250

Founded in Bristol in 1869, the Brecon house is a small dependent convent following the Vincentian Rule. The sisters run a retreat house. For further details please see entry for mother house, SC Bristol (England).

Habit: Blue coat and skirt with white blouse and SC cross
Membership: 3
Superior: Sister-in-charge

See also England and USA.

Community of Emmanuel Sisters and Brothers
Mixed

Emmanuel House
18 Royal Oak Road
Derwen Fawr
Swansea SA2 8ES
UK

Founded in 1968 as a lay community.

See also Jerusalem and the Middle East.

Society of the Sacred Cross
Mixed
RV   B   C

Tymawr Convent
Lydart
Monmouth
Gwent NP5 4RN
UK
Tel: 0600 860244

A contemplative community which is based upon the Cistercian life. The sisters have recently opened the novitiate to men in order to develop a double monastery.

Superior: The Rev'd Mother Gillian Mary, SSC

Community of St. Gregory
Mixed
B

St. Gregory's Retreat
Rhandirmwyn
Llandovery
Wales
Tel: 055 06 247

Affiliated with the monks at Elmore, the community is under the jurisdiction of the Archbishop of Wales. The way of life is inspired by St. Benedict and is centered on the Divine Office and space to give time for the leisure of reading and private prayer. Guests are encouraged to help in the work of the community. The retreat contains an oratory, a library, a shop and a small holding.

Resident Priest: The Rev'd Arthur Bell

Community of St. John the Evangelist
Women
RV   B   C

St. John's Priory
9 Methyr Mawr North
Bridgend
Mid Glamorgan
CF31 3NH
Wales
Tel: 0656 653822

The community was founded in 1912, not for any particular "good works" but to allow the sisters to lead hidden and dedicated lives of prayer. In 1985 the sisters moved to smaller accommodation in Bridgend and here they offer guests and small groups the opportunity of quiet and prayer in a noisy, bustling world.

Habit: Black habit with scapular, veil with white rim and white collar, CSJE cross and profession ring
Membership: 12
Superior: The Rev'd Mother Catherine Margaret, CSJE

ZIMBABWE

Order of the Holy Name
Women
RV   B

c/o St. Augustine's Mission
PO Penhalonga
Zimbabwe

Founded in 1935, the community is Benedictine in outlook but undertake an active ministry nursing, teaching, and in various parish-related works. The sisters run an orphanage for 36 children and make altar breads.

Habit: Light blue habit, white collar and dark blue veil; copper CZR cross inscribed with IHS
Membership: 8
Superior: Mother Isabella, CZR

Index

ANGLICAN RELIGIOUS ORDERS AND COMMUNITIES
ADDITIONAL, UPDATED, AND CORRECTED INFORMATION

PLEASE TYPE OR USE BLOCK CAPTITALS

NAME OF RELIGIOUS COMMUNITY: _____

_____

ADDRESS: _____

_____

_____

_____

TELEPHONE NUMBER: _____

FAX NUMBER: _____

CHURCH/AUTONOMOUS PROVINCE: _____

Please add the above details to your address list for:
RELIGIOUS ORDERS' DIRECTORY   ☐

DECADE OF EVANGELISM MAILINGS   ☐

Please note the following corrections to our entry in the
Religious Orders' Directory (I have attached the
amendments to this form)   ☐

Name _____

Position within community: _____

Return to: Religious Orders DIrectory
           Anglican Communion Office
           Partnership House
           157 Waterloo Road
           London SE1 8UT
           England